Parenting a Child with Asperger Syndrome

of related interest

Asperger Syndrome, the Universe and Everything
Kenneth Hall
Forewords by Ken P. Kerr and Gill Rowley
ISBN 1 85302 930 0

Asperger's Syndrome
A Guide for Parents and Professionals
Tony Attwood
Foreword by Lorna Wing
ISBN 1 85302 577 1

Freaks, Geeks and Asperger Syndrome
A User Guide to Adolescence
Luke Jackson
Foreword by Tony Attwood
ISBN 1 84310 098 3

The Self-Help Guide for Special Kids and their Parents
Joan Matthews and James Williams
ISBN 1 85302 914 9

Snapshots of Autism
A Family Album
Jennifer Overton
ISBN 1 84310 723 6

Raising a Child with Autism
A Guide to Applied Behaviour Analysis for Parents
Shira Richman
ISBN 1 84310 825 9

Parents' Education as Autism Therapists
Applied Behaviour Analysis in Context
Edited by Mickey Keenan, Ken P. Kerr and Karola Dillenburger
ISBN 1 85302 778 2

How to Live with Autism and Asperger Syndrome
Practical Strategies for Parents and Professionals
Chris Williams and Barry Wright
Illustrated by Olive Young
ISBN 1 84310 184 X

Parenting a Child with Asperger Syndrome

200 Tips and Strategies

Brenda Boyd

Jessica Kingsley Publishers
London and Philadelphia

First published in the United Kingdom in 2003
by Jessica Kingsley Publishers
116 Pentonville Road
London N1 9JB, UK
and
400 Market Street, Suite 400
Philadelphia, PA 19106, USA

www.jkp.com

Library of Congress Cataloging in Publication Data
A CIP catalog record for this book is available from the Library of Congress

British Library Cataloguing in Publication Data
A CIP catalogue record for this book is available from the British Library

ISBN-13: 978 1 84310 137 6
ISBN-10: 1 84310 137 8

Printed and Bound in Great Britain by
Athenaeum Press, Gateshead, Tyne and Wear

In memory of my father,
Garret Antony O'Reilly, 1920–1991

Acknowledgements

I would like to thank everyone who has helped me in the writing of this book, especially:

- My husband, Chris, for being my anchor, for all his great ideas, for the times he helped me see more clearly and for his patience through thick and thin.

- Christine, my daughter, for believing in me and for supporting me right from the start.

- My friend, Carol, for her suggestions and for helping me believe I had an important job to do.

- Maura, my sister, for steering me to make the book more practical than it might have been otherwise.

- 'Nana' Margaret, for painstakingly checking the final draft.

- And last but not least my son, Kenneth, for inspiring me with his positive and courageous attitude – and for giving me something to write a book about!

Contents

Appendices

How To Use
This Book in a Hurry

There are three ways to look quickly for ideas that might help you on a specific problem.

1. By looking through the Contents.

2. By turning to an entry under Common Problems A–Z (Chapter 3, pp.63–148).

    This chapter focuses on some common Asperger problems, and is arranged alphabetically.

3. By looking through the Tip Finder at the back of the book (pp.192–202).

    This is a quick list of all the ideas, tips and strategies contained throughout the entire book. They are numbered, which means that when you find the tip you are looking for, you can easily locate it in the main body of the book.

Introduction

Being a parent is one of the most important jobs in the world, and yet how do we learn to do it? For other important jobs we need formal training and qualifications, but in general we are just expected to *know* how to be a parent. Most of what we learn usually comes from watching others – in particular how our own parents raised us. Usually this works out fine, but when you have a child with Asperger Syndrome (AS) it can sometimes be hard to know which way to turn. The typical AS child presents us with all the usual parenting challenges – plus a whole lot of extra ones besides. AS parents tend to understand each other, because our experiences are often so similar. But it's next to impossible for anyone else to really understand, and this means you can end up feeling very alone.

I have two children, a daughter and a son. My daughter is now grown up and thankfully she has turned out to be a lovely, well-balanced person and a great friend. When she was a child she was easygoing and compliant and I found her quite easy to raise. But my son Kenneth was a different story right from the start.

When Kenneth was small, I seemed to have nothing but problems and worries with him, and for years no one could understand why. A lot of the problems weren't that unusual in a way, and sometimes I tried to reassure myself that plenty of other children were the same. But in my heart I knew this was something different. Kenneth's difficulties were much more extreme; plus he didn't seem to be growing out of them. From the outside he just looked like a spoilt, badly behaved and unhappy child, and I hated that. Sometimes I blamed myself and sometimes I blamed him. When, at the age of eight, he was finally diagnosed with Asperger Syndrome (or high functioning autism as it is also known), I had very mixed feelings. Part of me was sad and anxious for the future. Part of me was relieved that we now had an explanation. Overall, I found it a great help to get the diagnosis. But I still felt very alone and daunted by the task ahead. Nobody I knew seemed to understand. And worse still, nobody seemed to be able to give me the parenting advice I desperately needed.

Diagnosis often marks the end of a difficult and puzzling journey for parents. When we start to find out about Asperger Syndrome, it can help explain a lot. But of course diagnosis does not make the problems go away. We still have a very demanding job to do, and even the very best of 'ordinary' parenting strategies do not always work. Sometimes it can seem that even if you had the patience of a saint and the wisdom of Solomon all rolled into one, it still might not be enough!

Handling the needs and challenges of an AS child is a big responsibility and very hard work. There is no magic solution that is going to change that. This book is meant to serve as a sort of ideas toolbox rather than a quick fix. Hopefully you will be able to dip into it and find ideas to help you meet needs and handle specific behaviour issues as they come along. I hope you will find that at least some of the suggestions help to make life easier for you and your family.

How This Book is Organised

There are ideas, tips and strategies running throughout the main text of the book, each one numbered in sequence as it appears. They are all in Tip Boxes so they are easy to find. The book is arranged as follows.

I   Laying the Foundations (pp.15–38)

This chapter suggests ways to help the child with AS feel loved and accepted and explores some of the reasons why this can be so difficult to achieve. It also covers understanding, building self-esteem and reducing anxiety.

2 Bringing Out the Best in Your Child (pp.39–62)

This chapter explores the best approach for handling an AS child, and suggests some ways to help him learn social and emotional skills. It also includes ideas to encourage compliance and motivation and to deal with difficult moments.

3 Common Problems A–Z (pp.63–148)

This chapter focuses on some common Asperger problems one by one, exploring each of them in some detail and suggesting ways to handle them.

4 A Word of Personal Reflection (pp.149–152)

I have included here a few of my own thoughts on the experience of having an AS child. This includes what I have learned and 'A Report from Planet Asperger'.

Tip Finder (pp.192–202)

This is a quick list of all the ideas, tips and strategies contained throughout the entire book. They are all numbered, which means that once you find the tip you are looking for in the Tip Finder, you can easily locate it in the main body of the book.

A Word About Siblings

It is very easy for other children in the family to feel neglected when they have an AS brother or sister who needs a lot of time and attention. They can end up feeling resentful and it can seem to them as if they are being penalised for being better behaved and less demanding. It makes sense to allow all the children in the family to be included as much as possible in the ideas you are using with your AS child. Most of them would be appealing and helpful to any child. And some of them are good fun!

A Note to Carers Other Than Parents

Parents are usually the people with primary responsibility for taking care of their children. But other people can have a valuable role too, for example, grandparents, aunts, uncles, relatives, teachers, carers and friends. These people often do a great job in helping to love and care for children. So even though they are not actual parents, this book is addressed to them too.

A Word About Gender

For whatever reason, many more males than females are diagnosed with Asperger Syndrome. This is one of the reasons that I have referred to the child as 'he' throughout the book. The other reason is that it was easier. But of course everything in the book applies to Asperger girls just as much as to boys.

How I Refer to the Child

Throughout the book instead of talking about a 'child with Asperger Syndrome' I often refer to him as an 'AS child'. The reason for this is that my own son prefers this description and I hope it does not cause offence in any way.

I

Laying the Foundations

Looking After Yourself
Acceptance and Understanding
Building Self-Esteem
Reducing Anxiety

Looking After Yourself

The greatest need that any child has is the need for unconditional love. Parents realise this intuitively. We know that unconditional love is the most powerful force on earth. When a child feels safe, loved and accepted for who he is, it allows him to make healthy progress in every area of his life. Of course our job as parents is not only to love our children, but also to make sure they know at a deep level that they are loved. This is the foundation upon which we try to build all of our parenting.

With an AS child it can be very hard to get this vital foundation laid. There are a lot of reasons for this. For example, he tends to have a very unrealistic self-image; he suffers from a lot of anxiety; he has huge social problems; he is hard to motivate; and his behaviour can be very difficult to handle. All this gives him extreme problems in relating to the world. But it also means that even more than most, he needs to hear from his parents, loud and clear, the message that tells him: 'You will never stop me loving you.'

Later parts of this chapter will suggest specific ways in which we can lay this basic foundation for an AS child so he can go through life secure in the knowledge that he is safe, loved and accepted.

When you have an AS child you soon discover that he needs you to go the extra mile for him again and again. But there are some very good reasons why you need to look after yourself before you do anything else. When a child has Asperger Syndrome, it has a huge impact not only on his life but also on the life of the people around him, especially his parents. If we neglect ourselves, we gradually build up stress, resentment and anger which slowly simmer away, causing damage to our health. If this continues over an extended period of time we can gradually become burned out, exhausted and even physically ill. We can end up with nothing left to give and then everybody suffers. So, before you start to meet the needs of your AS child, first make sure your own needs are being met.

TIP BOX
Looking After Yourself

1   Keep yourself stocked up (the 'Freezer Tip!')

2   Get plenty of support

3   Don't take things personally

4   Don't neglect other areas of your life

5   Be realistic about tackling problems

6   Give yourself SMART goals

7   Let the strategies be 'on tap' not 'on top'

8   Try not to spoil him

9   Find someone to talk to

10   Let yourself off the hook

11   'Mind over matter!'

TIP # 1 Keep yourself stocked up (the 'Freezer Tip!')

Think of yourself as a freezer full of food! When you are well stocked up you have plenty to give, not only to your children but also to the other important people in your life, when they need it. The problem is that the more you give, the more your stock gradually runs down. If you don't keep filling it up again you will gradually have less and less to give and one day there might be nothing left. So keep an eye on the 'stock in your freezer'. Keep yourself filled up with what *you* need so you are in a position to give your children what *they* need.

Make a point of regularly doing things just for yourself: take some time off; go to the gym; have a bubble bath; go out for coffee with a friend; watch a video; go for a walk; listen to your favourite music. Just do whatever it takes to keep you feeling happy and nurtured. And if you find yourself feeling guilty, *don't!* Just tell yourself you are keeping the freezer well stocked so you have more to give to the people you love.

TIP # 2 Get plenty of support

It is worth putting the effort into establishing the best support network you can come up with. It is a great help if you have people you can rely upon to help out or give you some respite. Take up any offer of help you get from family or friends. There's no point in making a martyr of yourself by turning it down. Check with your local medical services, social services, charitable bodies, etc. to see what help may be available. If you can afford to pay for some extra help it could be a good investment in your health and peace of mind. Sometimes students are glad of the opportunity to look after your child for a few hours per week, especially if they are studying some aspect of child development. Try placing an advert in your local college or newspaper (but of course make sensible security checks when employing strangers).

TIP # 3 Don't take things personally

As parents we expect to put a lot of effort into *giving* love to all our children. But those moments when we feel 'loved back' are very special. They are a source of great joy and reassurance. Something that can be hard on AS parents is that they don't always feel as if they are 'loved back'.

It can be hurtful when you don't get the feedback you want from your child: the reassuring smile, the cuddle, the pleasant word; or, worse still, when he seems downright rude or hostile. It is important not to take things personally because your child doesn't mean them personally. No matter how he behaves, you know in your heart that he loves you and that he needs your love too.

TIP # 4 Don't neglect other areas of your life

Because AS children need so much time and energy, looking after them can end up almost taking over your life if you let it. It is easy to end up neglecting your other interests and pursuits. Try to keep things in balance by paying attention to your other relationships and interests as well.

TIP # 5 Be realistic about tackling problems

Sometimes there are so many difficult issues to address it can seem overwhelming. It is impossible to tackle everything at once, so how do you know where to start?

Step back and assess the situation realistically. Jot down a list of the problems as you see them and prioritise them on the basis of how urgently they need to be addressed. This will depend on things like the seriousness of the issue and how many problems it is causing for the child, for you, and for other people around him. It can be helpful to make this list along with a friend or partner.

A big advantage about this kind of realistic approach is that once you have decided to focus on the more urgent problems, you can give yourself a break and let some others go for the moment.

TIP # 6 Give yourself SMART goals

Don't expect too much of yourself or your child too quickly. When you are trying to make progress in any area, take it step by step. Give yourself a break by setting **SMART** goals. SMART means:

- **S**mall
- **M**easurable
- **A**chievable
- **R**ealistic
- **T**ime based.

For example, a non-SMART goal might be for your child to 'be more polite'. A SMART goal might be that he should 'greet three people politely over the course of the day'.

TIP # 7 Let the strategies be 'on tap' not 'on top'

Remember that tips and strategies are there to serve you, and not the other way around. So be flexible. If an idea works, and for as long as it works, go for it. But if an idea doesn't work or it doesn't feel right to you, just ignore it. Trust your judgement. You know your own child best. But also keep in mind that timing can make a difference: Sometimes an idea that does not work today might work in six months time and vice versa. So try things out; see what works for your child and follow your intuition.

TIP # 8 Try not to spoil him

It is a big mistake to overindulge any child by giving him too much of his own way and too many material things. When we do this, we make life more difficult for ourselves because we end up with a very demanding and and unpleasant child to deal with. But it is very easy to fall into the trap of 'spoiling' an AS child for various reasons. For example:

- We feel sorry for him when life is tough and we want to make it up to him.

- He is very demanding and insists that he gets what he wants, and it is easier to give in than stand up to him.

- We naturally want him to be happy and we feel guilty and responsible when we see him disappointed (sometimes even when his disappointment is totally unreasonable).

The fundamental reason for indulging a child is usually that we want him to be happy. The thing we need to keep in mind is that *overindulgence will never make him happy in the long run*. It will only give him a totally unrealistic view of life and set him up for a lot of misery and disappointment in the future. It is harder work to say 'no' sometimes, but it can ultimately be kinder for you and for the child.

One suggestion for when you feel like giving him a treat is to find a way to present it to him as a reward for good behaviour. For example, if he asks for a new video game, say something like: 'I'd really love to get you that game, and I think you deserve it as a reward for the effort you have made when you...'

TIP # 9 Find someone to talk to

Make sure you don't keep your feelings bottled up inside. You need to have at least one person you feel you can confide in and tell how you really feel. It could be perhaps a family member, your partner, a friend or a counsellor. The main thing is that you have the chance to let off steam sometimes. Talking really can help!

TIP # 10 Mums – let yourself off the hook

Mums in particular have a habit of feeling guilty unless they are putting themselves last. We need to let ourselves off the hook, because nobody else can do it for us. Look after yourself. It is not a selfish thing to do. Think of the advice given by airlines: 'In an emergency put on your own oxygen mask first before trying to help others.'

Remember: one of the most effective ways of loving a child is to *look after his mother*!

TIP # 11 'Mind over matter!'

To outsiders, AS children often come across as rude, gauche and arrogant. When their behaviour provokes a disapproving look or comment, the child is usually quite oblivious. But as parents we can pick up the vibes of disapproval and judgement all too easily. The next time you feel upset and embarrassed at how other people are judging you or your child, remember this: *'Those who mind don't matter and those who matter don't mind.'*

Acceptance and Understanding

It can be very hard for a child with AS to find acceptance in the world. He is forever 'getting it wrong' socially and breaking rules he didn't even know existed. And the world deals harshly with people who break the unwritten rules. It doles out cruel punishments such as ridicule, bullying and isolation. But even in the home it can be hard for the child to find acceptance. One reason for this is that his behaviour needs so much correction that he can end up feeling as if he hears nothing but criticism and judgement. Another reason is that parents sometimes have a negative attitude to the diagnosis of Asperger Syndrome and this can give a message of rejection to the child. The AS child needs and deserves to feel accepted and understood as a unique and valuable human being of whom Asperger Syndrome is an integral part. Here are some suggestions as to how we as parents can help to meet that need.

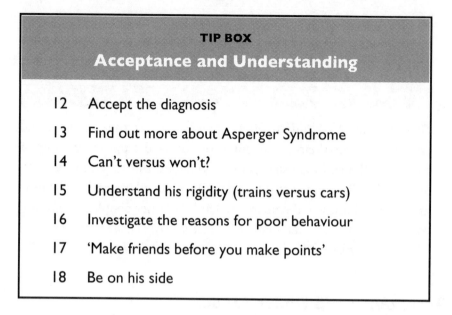

TIP # 12 Accept the diagnosis

If we are honest, very few parents welcome diagnosis with open arms. We say, for instance, that we don't want to 'label' our child and we tend to deny and resist for as long as we can. But we really need to be careful about what message this gives our children.

I have even heard it said that parents go through a period of *grieving* when they receive the diagnosis. Maybe this is a natural process, but if so we need to work our way through it, even if it is long and hard, so we can eventually come out the other end. We need to challenge ourselves with the fact that we are only grieving for an illusion – the illusion of the child we might have had. As we start to let go of this illusion, we become free to accept and rejoice in the wonderful child we do have.

Our AS children need us to be proud of them and accept them unconditionally, and this includes accepting their Asperger Syndrome. For to deny the AS is to deny the child, whereas to accept and embrace the AS is to accept and embrace the child.

TIP # 13 Find out more about Asperger Syndrome

Even though AS children are all unique, it can be quite an eye-opener to discover how much they have in common. Sometimes the more we find out about Asperger Syndrome, the more we can understand our own child. Knowledge is power and, after all, they do say that to understand is to forgive!

The first book most parents read to find out about Asperger Syndrome is Tony Attwood's (1998) book. It is a very good first port of call. When I first read it I remember thinking, 'How come this man knows my child so well?' There are lots of other excellent books available, and websites to explore as well (see Useful Websites and Bibliography at end of book). And you may also be able to link into a local support group. All these things can be very informative and can help you feel you are not alone.

At some point the child may also show an interest in finding out about Asperger Syndrome. If so, talk to him openly and calmly. Don't let him be afraid of the name. Make sure he knows that the word 'syndrome' is just an old-fashioned word meaning 'like' and that Mr Asperger was an Austrian man who was very interested in children like him. Let him read books if he wants to and encourage the rest of the family to take an interest and become involved as well. It can be fun to discuss AS traits and think about who else in the family might have them. Search the internet. Find out what famous people are thought to have AS traits. It can be a learning process for everyone!

TIP # 14 Can't versus won't?

It can often be very hard to tell whether a child with AS is capable of something or whether it is not fair to expect it from him. As you start to understand more about AS, it can help you at least start to unravel what he can't do from what he won't do.

Remember that children with AS often have difficulties with things that ordinary children take for granted. In many situations they need extra help and guidance where you wouldn't expect it. So don't automatically assume the child understands things and knows what is expected just because it would be obvious to other children.

TIP # 15 Understand his rigidity (trains versus cars)

One of the key features about AS children that we need to get to grips with is their rigidity: they dislike change and need a lot of routine. They tend to have very fixed ideas and can be obsessive and stubborn. Rigidity also helps account for many of their more baffling and maddening traits. (See p.110 for a fuller discussion about rigidity.) Why is it that people with Asperger Syndrome insist on being so rigid? We know they feel safest when life seems predictable and certain. Perhaps being rigid gives them the order that they crave and helps them make sense of a world they find chaotic and unpredictable.

The analogy of 'trains versus cars' gives us some insight into what Asperger rigidity is like. This idea compares the Asperger mind to a train on a train track, as opposed to the typical mind, which is more like a car on a road. The main difference between a train track and a road is that train tracks are rigid. When a train starts off on its journey it has to stay on course in a predictable way until it gets to where it originally set out for. Cars on the other hand are not so predictable. Car drivers see more possibilities. They can easily change lanes, turn off the road, stop or change direction. This analogy helped explain a lot of things about my son that had been a puzzle to me. It also helped me understand that he was usually not just being rigid and stubborn on purpose. It is genuinely difficult for children with Asperger Syndrome to be flexible.

TIP # 16 Investigate the reasons for poor behaviour

Later in the book there are lots of ideas to help tackle specific behaviour problems, but it is always worth trying to understand what lies behind poor behaviour as well. There are usually several possibilities to consider:

1. *He is testing the boundaries.* Sometimes when a child behaves badly it just means he is testing the boundaries. All children do this from time to time, and the AS child is no exception. At these times we can help him best by being kind but firm. (See Tip 55.) He needs to know that there are fair and clear boundaries, and that we care enough to protect those boundaries. He may not like it at the time, but it will ultimately help him feel more secure.

2. *He is upset or frustrated.* But of course it's not always just a matter of testing boundaries. Poor behaviour from an AS child is often his way of expressing a grievance. He may be 'communicating in code' that he is upset and frustrated. If so we need to try and find out what his grievance is, as well as whether it is a 'genuine grievance' or an 'AS grievance'.

3. *He has a 'genuine grievance'.* If the child has some genuine grievance, it is better that we know about it. At least then we can take steps to address it. Look at possibilities such as:

   ○ Is he under undue stress at school or for some other reason?
   ○ Is he feeling very disappointed about something?
   ○ Might he have been teased or bullied?
   ○ Has he been deliberately 'set up' or provoked in some way, for example, by other children?
   ○ Is there any other factor that you can think of?

4. *He has an 'AS grievance'.* Sometimes you discover that poor behaviour has been prompted by what I call an 'AS grievance'; in other words, something that is very important to the child, but seems silly, minor or unreasonable from the outside. His behaviour is way out of proportion to the grievance. As an extreme example, the AS child throws a heavy punch and injures another child. It turns out that this incident was provoked by a teasing remark about his

favourite football team. Yet the AS child is unwilling to accept any responsibility. (If so, see Tip 17 below.)

TIP # 17 'Make friends before you make points'

As with any child, the goal is always to 'love the child but challenge the behaviour'. But this it is not easy to do when he is being completely unreasonable, or complaining about an 'Asperger grievance' (see Tip 16). At such times it can be tempting to try and use logic to show him he is wrong or unreasonable, but it probably won't work. We have to accept that *for the moment* this is his reality. At this point, he is sincerely convinced that his grievance is genuine and his behaviour was justified.

Over time we can do a lot to help the AS child by gradually challenging his thinking, but the key is that the timing needs to be right. He needs to be feeling calm, confident and happy in order to be receptive. While he is still upset it is completely the wrong time to argue with him, as he is likely to be more rigid than usual and will probably just become more entrenched.

Concentrate most of your effort into giving him a message of unconditional acceptance. Sound sympathetic to his grievance without either judging it or condoning his behaviour. If he can trust you to be on his side no matter what, he will be more open and receptive to what you have to say to him later, when the time is right. Remember you need to *make friends before you make points*.

TIP # 18 Be on his side

Do all you can to make sure the child is in no doubt that you and he are on the same side. Being on his side includes being warm and accepting, taking an interest in what is important to him and listening to him without judgement (see also Tip 52, Be an ally; Tip 107, Empathic listening).

This doesn't mean accepting unacceptable behaviour, of course. But when we are correcting him, we need to do our best to separate the child from the behaviour. It is crucial that he starts to get the message that it is the *behaviour*, not him, that we don't like. Tell him in words that you and he are on the same side and that in a family everybody is supposed to be on the same side. Don't assume he knows these things without being told. He needs you to *tell as well as show* him that you care about him, you value his company, you like him, you enjoy his sense of humour and you sympathise with his difficulties.

Building Self-Esteem
The importance of healthy self-esteem

A good healthy self-esteem is vital in any child and helps him in just about every area of his life. Poor self-esteem can manifest itself in all sorts of ways, including withdrawal and anger, and can even lead to depression.

THE DIFFICULTY WITH THE AS CHILD

When an AS child has low self-esteem, it is not always easy to recognise because of how he comes across. For example, when he seems aloof, arrogant and opinionated, it is hard to imagine that this kind of attitude may be masking a low self-esteem. But when you think about it, people who are secure and happy don't usually feel the need to behave this way. One of the reasons why a child with AS might have problems with his self-esteem is that he tends to have a very unrealistic self-image to start with. Often he is a perfectionist and doesn't see his own strengths and weaknesses clearly at all. He vacillates between grandiose ideas of his capabilities and miserable disappointment when he fails to come up to his own standards (see Perfectionism, Tips 148–54). Also, it is easy to imagine how his self-esteem must suffer simply on account of the difficulties that Asperger Syndrome typically presents. It must be very dispiriting at times to go through life feeling misunderstood and confused by the world.

How we can help

There is a lot we can do to help shape a positive self-image in our AS children. It is bound to be a slow and difficult task, but it is very worthwhile. Here are some self-esteem building tips.

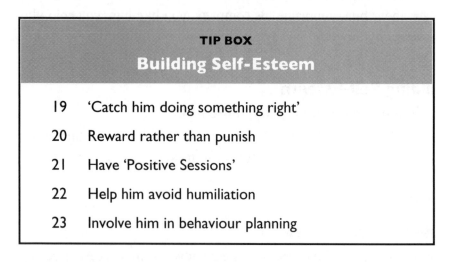

TIP BOX

Building Self-Esteem

19   'Catch him doing something right'

20   Reward rather than punish

21   Have 'Positive Sessions'

22   Help him avoid humiliation

23   Involve him in behaviour planning

TIP # 19 'Catch him doing something right'

Too often as parents we forget the power of praise. Instead of looking for things to praise in our children, we wait till we notice them doing something wrong and then criticise them for it. Yet praise is a powerful motivator. It builds self-esteem by letting children know 'You're doing OK.' And the AS child needs this feedback more than most. Train yourself to look for opportunities to give him warm, encouraging feedback on his behaviour, on the effort he is making and on his progress.

THE MOST EFFECTIVE WAY TO PRAISE AN AS CHILD

It is important to get it right when praising a child with AS, because he may absolutely *hate* praise that seems too gushing or general. He will usually be most comfortable with praise that seems genuine but not overemotional. A strategy that works well for praising an AS child is to use the formula *'See-Feel-Name'*.

- *See.* Say what you see. For example, 'I see you have allowed your sister to join in with your game.'

- *Feel.* Describe what you feel: 'I am very pleased to see you two playing together nicely.'

- *Name.* Give a name to the behaviour you are praising: 'That's what I call being a kind and friendly brother.'

TIP # 20 Reward rather than punish

Try to base your approach on *'Improvement and Reward'* and think of punishment only as a last resort. And remember that rewards do not need to be material or expensive. A reward can also be a 'Well done', a favourite meal, a hug, an outing or even the one-to-one attention of an adult chatting and listening to him.

TIP # 21 Have 'Positive Sessions'

'Positive Sessions' are family fun times when you set aside a certain amount of time for talking only about positive things. The rules are:

- Only one person speaks at a time.

- Everyone else listens.

- You can talk about anything at all, as long as it is positive.

Openers could be for example:

- I enjoyed my ice cream after dinner.

- I really appreciated it when you tidied your toys.

- The visit to the cinema was good fun.

TIP # 22 Help him avoid humiliation

Every child in the world hates to be humiliated and will do what he can to avoid it. Children with Asperger Syndrome must suffer more than their fair share of humiliation and this can be very tough on them. Look for ways to help him avoid humiliation. For example:

- Let him experience plenty of successes by putting him in 'win–win' situations. This means that sometimes it is better to avoid things when you know he will find them too hard.

- Don't draw attention to his mistakes too much.

- When he does get it wrong, show him how to make amends and encourage him to think: 'How could we do it differently next time?'

- When there is conflict, don't back him into a corner. Try to offer him a face-saving way out.

TIP # 23 Involve him in behaviour planning

When a behaviour issue arises, rather than always imposing a solution or ultimatum, try presenting the problem to him as something you and he can work on *together*. For example, you could say something like: 'When your aunt was visiting today your behaviour seemed rude. I know you didn't mean to be rude, but it looked very unfriendly when she said "Hi, how are you?" and you just walked on past and went to your room. I'd like us to talk about some ways you might behave differently next time so you don't seem rude.'

Then leave space for some feedback from him and discuss or role play some possible 'friendly responses'. This kind of approach sometimes works because it can help him feel respected and lets him know you value his ideas and opinions.

Reducing Anxiety
The link between Asperger Syndrome and anxiety

In order to lay a good solid foundation for a child with AS, not only do we need to make sure he feels safe, loved and accepted, but we also need to take steps to reduce his anxiety levels. The experts tell us that people with Asperger Syndrome are prone to anxiety. We all suffer from anxiety and stress at times and so we know how it can affect us. When we are anxious or under a lot of stress, we can't cope with life as well as usual. We may not be able to concentrate or sleep properly. We tend to be unreasonable and irritable. We might have trouble eating, perhaps overeating, perhaps undereating. We can become a bit obsessive, getting upset at small and trivial things and we tend to get difficulties way out of proportion.

When you think about it, we see an awful lot of these exact symptoms in our AS children and this should give us some idea of the amount of anxiety they have to suffer on a daily basis.

The cause

The amount of anxiety that people generally experience depends on their personality as well as external factors. Some people are just more prone to anxiety than others. We've all come across people who seem to sail through life and cope with whatever comes their way without a care in the world. Then at the opposite end of the spectrum there are people who are burdened by anxiety no matter what's going on around them. In an extreme case a person might become anxious over a very minor decision: which of two items of clothing to wear for example. It is as if their anxiety comes from within, even though they rationalise it by blaming some external factor. This end of the personality spectrum is where we find our AS children.

'Asperger anxiety'

What causes anxiety in an AS child? Sometimes there is a clear external reason. For example, the child may be suffering from bullying either at school or elsewhere. Other times the reason is obscure and hard to understand from the outside. I think of these instances as *Asperger anxiety*, which we just have to accept.

I remember once being in a shop with my son when he was about nine years old. I had brought him there to choose some colouring pencils for the start of the new school term. He seemed to be spending absolutely ages looking at all the different pencils in an intense and obsessive way. While he was still choosing, we met a lady who was a friend of ours. After chatting to me for a bit, she tried to engage Kenneth in friendly conversation by asking questions – things like what colour pencils he liked and when the new school term would be starting. There was no reply, just silence. In vain she tried repeatedly to get a response from him until all of a sudden he barked out at her in a very loud and angry voice, 'Be silent immediately. Can you not see I am trying to concentrate?'

I can see the funny side of it now, and I'm sure you've had many similar embarrassing experiences. But it was puzzling too. Why did he have to be so rude and unpleasant? Was he deliberately trying to cause offence? Could he not see the lady was only trying to be friendly? Could he not see that he had caused embarrassment? It's easier looking back to see that the answer was no. He literally didn't see these things because of his Asperger 'mind blindness'. But another big factor was his anxiety.

Why was he anxious? Part of it must have been the social aspect of the situation; being in the shop and meeting someone he wasn't expecting to meet. But it was only later that I understood that the task of choosing the pencils was making him anxious too. Even though I'd seen this kind of thing before, I hadn't figured out that making choices can sometimes make a person with Asperger Syndrome anxious. It's interesting to wonder why this should be so. Perhaps they are worried about getting things wrong or making a wrong decision. We can't ever know for sure.

How we can help

Some key strategies that can help us manage anxiety levels in our children are to:

- understand and make allowances
- provide order, structure and predictability.

TIP BOX

Reducing Anxiety

Understand and make allowances

24   Be aware of 'hidden anxiety'

25   Investigate the reasons

26   Aim for an optimum level of anxiety

Provide order, structure and predictability

27   Time any changes carefully

28   Use a noticeboard

29   Use a timer or stopwatch

30   Use visual aids

31   Laminate the visual aids

A few other suggestions

32   Exercise

33   Distraction

34   'Jammy Days'

Understand and make allowances

TIP # 24 Be aware of 'hidden anxiety'

Sometimes Asperger Syndrome is referred to as a 'hidden disability' because of how the difficulties are not obvious. But we need to be on the lookout for 'hidden anxiety' too, because from the outside many typical Asperger traits look nothing like anxiety. They can look more like the opposite, even to parents at times. Additionally, some traits become more extreme when the child is anxious.

Let's think a bit about how AS traits appear to the outside world. I found an interesting summary on the Asperger 'diagnosis card' I got when Kenneth was first diagnosed. This is a small card, only about the size of a business card, which you can carry in a purse or wallet. It is interesting because it is designed to be read by someone who knows absolutely nothing about the condition and so it has to come straight to the point. Here is what it says:

> What is Asperger Syndrome?
>
> Asperger Syndrome is a disability which in some ways is similar to autism. People with Asperger Syndrome generally look and sound normal. They have difficulties in the areas of social understanding and social communication. They can appear rude, gauche and arrogant and can behave in odd, eccentric and unpredictable ways.
>
> Asperger Syndrome can affect people from all walks of life and with various degress of intelligence from moderate learning difficulties to intellectually gifted. Please be patient, they do not mean to offend.

It's sobering, isn't it, to think that our children come across in such an unendearing way. 'Rude, gauche, arrogant and offensive' is not most people's picture of anxiety. And yet as parents we know in our hearts that however appearances look, our children must suffer from a lot of anxiety, even if it is hidden. The problem is that the world won't make allowances for difficulties that are hidden, which makes it even more important for us as parents to do so.

TIP # 25 Investigate the reasons

What triggers anxiety? It's worth trying to understand so we can do our best to help, even though it's not possible to tell in every situation. Keep in mind that one of the most difficult things for AS children is dealing with things that are unfamiliar and unpredictable. To try and understand what is causing anxiety, we can ask ourselves questions:

- What has been going on in his life recently? Have there been any changes?

- Has he recently changed class?

- Has his routine changed?

- Is he ill, run down or especially tired?

- Has someone new come into his life?

- Might there be anything going on that you're not aware of? Bullying at school? Sensory difficulties?

- Is there any kind of pattern?

- Is there anything he seems to find especially difficult?

- Might there be bullying going on at school? (See p.117)

Sometimes the cause is quite specific. At other times there's no obvious cause at all and we need to accept that it is simply 'Asperger anxiety'. The world can be a confusing, hostile and unpredictable world for an AS child. Even if we don't always understand, we can do a lot simply by making sure he knows we are on his side.

TIP # 26 Aim for an optimum level of anxiety

As parents we hate to see our children anxious, cross and miserable and we realise they are more vulnerable than they seem. Naturally we long to help and protect them, but at the same time we know it's a bad idea to overprotect them. It can be hard to get the balance right.

It's good to remember that ultimately anxiety is part of life. Even though too much anxiety can be paralysing, a little bit of anxiety can be useful when it spurs us on to do things we might not otherwise attempt. At the *optimum level of anxiety* the child will feel comfortable enough to try something new and in the process learn that he can deal with difficult situations. The goal is to manage anxiety, not eliminate it. Realistically this is going to be an ongoing, long-term process.

We can do a lot to help our children make sense of the world and make life more predictable for them. But they also need to learn that life can't always be controlled or predicted. Sometimes things don't go according to plan – and that's OK too.

Provide order, structure and predictability

TIP # 27 Time any changes carefully

Keep in mind that even a minor change often makes the AS child very anxious. Try to introduce any kind of change, even alterations to his schedule, at a time when you are both feeling relaxed, and give him plenty of advance warning if you can.

TIP # 28 Use a noticeboard

If you don't already have a noticeboard in your home, consider getting one. It can be used as a point of reference for the child, to display information that will help make the world a bit more predictable for him, for example: ground rules, schedules, contracts, star charts, etc. Make sure it is placed somewhere accessible to him, such as the kitchen, living area or maybe in his bedroom, so that he can refer to it himself when he needs to.

TIP # 29 Use a timer or stopwatch

Kitchen timers are generally available quite easily and cheaply and stopwatches can be purchased in sports shops. These items are a great investment for the AS child and can be a great help in giving him the structure and predictability that he needs. He may find a reassuring certainty in hearing the loud beep telling him the time is up. And apart from that they can be great fun to play with! Timers can be useful in many situations, for example:

- You need to settle down within the next two minutes.

- I want to have 20 minutes of peace without you interrupting me and then I will play a game with you. (If he interrupts, start the 20 minutes over again!)

- When you have done 15 minutes of homework then you can watch TV.

- You can read in bed for ten minutes and then the light must go out.

- Let's see if you can keep the ball bouncing for three minutes without stopping.

TIP # 30 Use visual aids

If we can help an AS child to know and remember what is expected of him, he will find it easier to make sense of the world and it will relieve some of his anxiety. Most AS children are visual thinkers, so it makes sense to provide them with plenty of visual aids for this purpose. A visual aid can be as simple as a quick written reminder or it can be a complicated and colourful display. Each child is completely different as to how visual aids might help him: whether it be a behaviour contract, ground rules, schedule, meal planner, or something else. You will know best what to try with your own child. But the principle is simply this: *The child with Asperger Syndrome usually learns and remembers far more from what he sees than from what he hears.*

There are endless ways in which this very important principle can be used and it can be fun to use your imagination to see what you can come up with. For example, make the visual aid more appealing by incorporating your child's special interest into it, or decorate it with stickers or drawings of his favourite cartoon character.

TIP # 31 Laminate the visual aids

Small, not too expensive laminating machines can be purchased at office supply shops. Although laminating is a bit of a luxury, it is very satisfying to have your visual aids laminated. For one thing they look much more attractive and appealing, and they are also more durable. If you use a suitable marker pen, the visual aid can then be wiped and reused again and again.

A few other suggestions

TIP # 32 Exercise

Exercise can be a great 'stress buster'. Sometimes when your child is anxious, it can calm him down if he gets out for a walk or engages in any kind of vigorous exercise, for example, playing, running or swimming.

TIP # 33 Distraction

Distract an anxious child into something he finds absorbing or interesting, based on something he is familiar and comfortable with. For example, give him a new colouring book or word search based on his special interest.

TIP # 34 'Jammy Days'

Every now and again let him have a 'Jammy Day' when he is allowed to slouch about in his pyjamas all day and do what he wants (within reason!). When you see him getting getting overanxious, schedule in a Jammy Day for him to look forward to.

2

Bringing Out the Best in Your Child

Bridging the Social and Emotional Gap
The Best Approach
Encouraging Compliance and Motivation
Dealing with Difficult Moments

Bridging the Social and Emotional Gap
'Teaching' social and emotional skills

Social and emotional difficulties have a profound influence on the life of a child with Asperger Syndrome. They affect his ability to behave and relate to other people in a successful and socially acceptable way. Outsiders often take offence at typical Asperger behaviour, even though they may not be able to put their finger on exactly why. They may label the child as rude or badly brought up. Yet often the child will not have had the slightest intention of causing any offence.

If we are blessed with good social and emotional skills our relationships with the world run smoothly: we know how to put people at their ease and make them feel comfortable. We consider their feelings and take them into account. But of course to do this we first need to be able to imagine those feelings, which puts the child with Asperger Syndrome at a huge disadvantage.

One of his major difficulties is what is sometimes called *'mind blindness'*, which basically means that he finds it very difficult to empathise or imagine the perspective of other people. This makes relationships incredibly difficult. It is hard to play successfully with other children when you don't have the 'social antennae' that they have. The AS child is not good at judging who is a real friend, and other children can be very hurtful. Parents worry terribly about these things. Our children are very vulnerable and we long to help them. We know that in the long run, if a person makes life uncomfortable for those around him, he can end up unpopular, disliked and alienated. It can ultimately even blight his career prospects.

When we have children, we expect to have to teach them many things: how to dress themselves, cross the road safely, feed themselves and so on. We don't normally expect to have to 'teach' them emotional and social skills. And yet, if an AS child is to learn these crucial skills, he *needs* to be taught. Ultimately our goal is to help develop his social and emotional awareness and understanding. But to do this we first have to try and understand his perspective and identify his blind spots.

The conflict between social skills and honesty

One of the reasons that children find concepts such as manners so difficult is that sometimes manners mean not being strictly honest. There can be a conflict between telling other people the truth and pleasing them. When this happens, 'normal' people often choose to tell a white lie rather than cause offence. Most of us accept such little deceits as part of how society operates. The fact that we use terms such as 'white lie' indicates that we think of them as harmless. The way we see it, sometimes it is worth sacrificing a little bit of honesty so that things run smoothly. Normally we don't even think about this very much. It just happens. So at times we say things that aren't quite true for the sake of making the other person comfortable. We don't say what's really on our mind. We know when it's the right time to 'hold our tongue'. We engage in small talk even when we are not really interested.

People with Asperger Syndrome do not operate like this at all, which means they sometimes 'rub us up the wrong way'. They are naive in the sense that they literally may not see the point of being anything other than honest and direct in all circumstances. They don't appreciate subtle concepts such as the 'white lie'. This can be very challenging to other people, but from the Asperger perspective it would be unnatural to behave in any other way.

TIP BOX

Bridging the Social and Emotional Gap

35   Appreciate his honesty as a very special attribute

36   Identify his blind spots

Developing his awareness: some techniques to try

37   Prompting and discussion

38   Use feedback to fill in the 'empathy gap'

Developing his awareness: some activities and games to try

39   An Emotions Book

40   A figures of speech project

41   Role play

42   Detective games

43   Teach him degrees of emotions

44   Expand his 'emotion vocabulary'

Play and social skills: some ideas to try

45   Enlist a buddy

46   Playdates

47   Let him be scorekeeper

48   Follow My Leader

49   Turn taking

50   Internet connections

TIP # 35 Appreciate his honesty as a very special attribute

Often the 'rude' behaviour of a child with Asperger Syndrome is really just honest behaviour. Honesty and directness are very much a part of Aspergers and even if we could, we don't want to stop our children being who they are.

Looked at positively, it is very rare and refreshing to come across the lack of hypocrisy and pretence which is so typical with Asperger Syndrome. It is certainly a challenge anyway! With an AS child at least you should always know exactly where you stand! There won't be much brushed under the carpet. There is no doubt that it is easier to be around people who have the opposite type of personality, the 'people pleasers' who tell us only what we want to hear. But on the other hand we do have a lot to learn from the honesty of AS children.

TIP # 36 Identify his blind spots

Before we can help the AS child, we need to try and identify what it is he does and doesn't understand, because it's very easy to assume he understands more than he does. It makes sense to think long and hard about where the gaps are in his awareness and understanding.

Recent research indicates that more than 90 per cent of social interaction consists of *non-verbal communication*, so this is clearly an extremely important skill. And yet it is probably safe to start off by assuming that this entire area of communication is beyond the awareness and understanding of the typical AS child. Most of us are intuitively good at non-verbal communication. We start to learn it intuitively when we are young. But this important learning process doesn't happen in the normal way for the child with Asperger Syndrome. His difficulty with non-verbal communication affects vast areas of his life including:

- his ability to read body language
- his awareness of unwritten social rules
- other subtle skills.

BODY LANGUAGE

Reading body language is a fascinating skill. We have the intuitive ability to 'read' other people's moods and intentions without their needing to tell us in words. How we do this is by picking up and interpreting all sorts of subtle non-verbal clues that they are giving out. Even more fascinating is the fact that this complex level of communication all goes on subconsciously.

But for the AS child it is the complete opposite. To take a simple example, most of us would find it easy to 'tell' if someone 'looked bored'. How do we do this? By 'reading' clues such as the expression on their face, the look in their eyes, their posture and gestures, or perhaps the tone of their voice. Yet even this simple example requires complex skills in non-verbal communication that the AS child does not naturally possess. To him non-verbal communication is a bit like a foreign language.

SOCIAL RULES

There are many unwritten and complex rules in society which are assumed by most of us and which help communication to run smoothly and effectively; for example, we generally defer to people in positions of authority. Once again, most of us start to learn these rules without even having to try when we are very young, but the AS child has little natural awareness of them.

OTHER SUBTLE SKILLS

Context awareness

He has little appreciation of different contexts and how they affect communication. This means he will tend to speak to everyone in the same direct way, which can often be seen as inappropriate.

Tact

He doesn't know much about tact and so he may see no reason why he shouldn't tell Granny he wishes she would go home, if that is how he feels.

Literal interpretation

He also has a tendency to take things such as figures of speech literally. This can lead to some funny situations at times, but it can also cause him problems of confusion and misunderstanding.

Developing his awareness: some techniques to try

TIP # 37 Prompting and discussion

PROMPTING

The AS child tends to act out his emotions rather than expressing them and has only limited awareness of his own emotional state. Coaching and prompting can help to develop his awareness. It can feel a bit strange at the start. After all you don't usually have to 'teach' children emotions. But it gets easier as you get used to it.

- Overact your own body language to show him how you feel.

- Tell him the rules in words. For example: 'When an adult is travelling with us in the car it is normally regarded as rude if a child refuses to allow him to sit in the front seat.'

- Talk openly and calmly to him about his emotions. Prompt him with the words he needs to express their reality. For example, 'When…happened that must have made you feel very angry (sad, happy, etc.)'. Ask leading questions if need be.

DISCUSSION

An important message for an AS child to hear and understand is as follows: *Every person (including you!) deserves to be treated well. This means you should treat other people the same way you would hope to be treated.*

Talk openly about how people deserve to be treated. Here are some questions and issues you could bring up during talks with your child or children:

- How do (each of) you like to be treated?

- How do you hate to be treated?

- Can you think of some examples of each of these?

- Who deserves to be treated well (e.g. sister, friend, Mum, Dad, etc.)?

Encourage discussion in the family about some of the subtle concepts that he does not easily understand such as:

- intentional and unintentional hurt (see Appendix 11)

- teasing and banter (see Appendix 12)

- bullying (see Appendices 13 and 14).

TIP # 38 Use feedback to help fill the 'empathy gap'

Remember he finds it very hard to put himself into the shoes of other people, so look out for everyday opportunities to tell him *in words* how you are feeling, using a calm, matter-of-fact voice. Also talk to him about how other people might be feeling, because he will not intuitively guess these things.

Explain to him how what he says or does can affect how other people feel. For example, if he gives you a hug, tell him very clearly, for instance: 'That made me feel good… When you give me a hug, it makes me feel so good.' Or if his behaviour is getting out of line, don't expect him to pick up subtle hints that you are not happy. Say it in words very clearly, for example: 'I am getting very cross' or 'When you throw your toys around the room that makes me very cross.'

Developing his awareness: some activities and games to try

TIP # 39 An Emotions Book

Make a special Emotions Book to help you explore emotions with the child. Have in it, for example, happy pages, sad pages, angry pages, frightened pages. Stick in or draw appropriate pictures, stories or words. Make lists of things that make you happy, things that make you angry, and so on. (Things that make you happy could include, for instance, chocolate bars and computer games.)

'Interview' friends and family and find out what makes them happy, sad, etc. This will help help him understand that different things make different people happy. (See Appendix 5, for some ideas on making an Emotions Book.)

TIP # 40 A figures of speech project

Make a family collection of figures of speech and put them into a notebook. Have everyone look out for examples and share them with the rest of the family:

- Rate them for funniness.

- Talk about what they actually mean and how you might translate them.

- Draw funny pictures of the figures of speech (for example, 'Mrs. Jones has green fingers').

TIP # 41 Role play

The child may enjoy role playing and it can allow him to try taking on the perspective of another person in a safe and fun way. There are unlimited ways in which it can be used. For example, replay situations that happened earlier and explore different ways in which they might have been handled. Have fun role playing telephone calls and social situations.

TIP # 42 Detective games

Turn down the sound on a TV show or soap opera and see how much you can guess about what is going on and how the characters are feeling just from the non-verbal communication: facial expression, gestures, and so on.

Cut out some photos of people from magazines and discuss how much you can guess about them just from the photo: their age, occupation, what they might be doing, how they might be feeling and why, etc.

TIP # 43 Teach him degrees of emotion

AS children are often only aware of the more extreme and straightforward emotions and tend to form simplistic opinions of people. For example, they are either 'happy' or 'sad' and, to them, other people might be either 'nice' and 'kind', or 'horrible' and 'yucky'.

Encourage them to be aware of degrees in between by using some kind of *simple visual code*. For example, if he says he is happy, you could ask 'How happy?' To indicate 'a tiny little bit happy' the code could be to put his hands quite close together. To indicate 'extremely happy', he could put them as far apart as they will go. You can then show him that there are degrees in between the two extremes.

TIP # 44 Expand his 'emotion vocabulary'

Explore some new and interesting words for expressing emotions: delighted, apprehensive, terrified, disappointed, furious, dismayed. Pick out some examples from the Emotion Vocabulary list in Appendix 7 and talk about what kind of situations might lead people to feel these emotions.

Play and social skills: some ideas to try

TIP # 45 Enlist a buddy

If you can, have at least one special adult in the child's life who will take an interest in him, play with him and help to teach him the skills he needs. This may be a friend or relation, or perhaps a student who might be glad to help out once a week for some extra pocket money.

TIP # 46 Playdates

Set up supervised playdates that you are pretty sure will be successful; for example, where the other child or children are likely to get along with your child. Make them reasonably structured and predictable so the AS child knows details such as when he is expected to arrive and leave, who will be there, what he is expected to do, and what is likely to happen.

TIP # 47 Let him be scorekeeper

If he has difficulties playing team games, he might enjoy being the scorekeeper or referee. This can also encourage him to observe the game and learn the rules (though you may need to steer him away from being too rigid and taking it far too seriously).

TIP # 48 Follow My Leader

Play the game 'Follow My Leader' whereby everyone observes what the 'Leader' does closely and copies it exactly (e.g. march along, clap hands, jump up and down, go round in a circle, etc.). The AS child might feel confident to take part because the rules are very simple and clear.

TIP # 49 Turn taking

He may need to have the concept of taking turns very clearly and patiently explained to him. He needs to understand not only how it works, but also how it is fair to everyone. Even when he does understand at an intellectual level, he may still need a lot of practice and encouragement as well. Find lots of simple fun examples; for instance: 'You have a turn at being "Leader" for five minutes, then your brother has a turn for five minutes.'

TIP # 50 Internet connections

He may enjoy making internet contacts and having e-mail penpals as a way of connecting with other people who have similar interests, or who have Asperger Syndrome.

The Best Approach

This section contains general tips on the best way to approach a child with Asperger Syndrome so as to bring out the best in him.

TIP BOX

The Best Approach

51	Be calm and relaxed
52	Be an ally
53	Communicate clearly
54	Approach discipline positively
55	Be kind yet firm
56	Give feedback
57	Be flexible
58	Think ahead
59	Present a united front
60	Choose your battles
61	Choose your timing
62	Have a sense of humour

TIP # 51 Be calm and relaxed

Any child, especially an AS child, responds best to a calm, relaxed approach, but of course it is hard to change your basic temperament if this style does not come easily to you. However, it is possible to make small changes that can help you become more relaxed: borrow a book from the library about relaxation; take up yoga; listen to a relaxing tape; have a massage; meditate; pray; or do whatever it is that helps you feel calm.

TIP # 52 Be an ally

Even when there are behaviour and discipline problems, most children know deep down that their parents are on their side. But you can't necessarily assume this with an AS child. He may sincerely come to the conclusion that you are against him just because, for example, you don't give him what he wants or you are trying to improve his behaviour.

Look for ways to make sure he knows that his parents are allies, no matter what. He may need to hear in words some things that most children don't usually need to be told: that you are his ally and friend; that it is your *job* as parent to help him improve his behaviour; that the reason you don't give him everything he wants is that you love him so much you don't want to do things that will be bad for him in the future (see also Tip 18, Be on his side).

TIP # 53 Communicate clearly

Remember it is not fair to expect an AS child to understand subtlety. Help him to understand what you are trying to communicate by reflecting the way he communicates, that is, honestly, clearly and unambiguously. Don't hint or leave any room for doubt. For example, if you want him to put on his coat, don't say 'Are you not cold?' or 'What about putting on your coat?' or even 'Would you *like* to put your coat on?' Instead say something very clear like 'You must put on your coat' or 'Please put on your coat.'

Tell him specifically and calmly what behaviour is expected of him and what are the consequences of his behaviour choices. You can't assume he knows unless it is spelt out to him. Be as consistent as you can and let him know when he is 'crossing the line'.

TIP # 54 Approach discipline positively

Rules of thumb are:

- 'Catch him doing something right' (see Tip 19).

- In general, ignore as much bad behaviour as you can and focus instead on the good behaviour.

- Use sanctions only as last resort.

Although the AS child benefits from clear rules and a structured approach to discipline, be careful not to overdo it. It is important to have fun with your child too. Keep in mind: *Rules without relationship mean rebellion* (see also Tip 23, Involve him in behaviour planning).

TIP # 55 Be kind yet firm

When an AS child knows there are very clear and firm boundaries, this can help him feel safe and secure. Remember that being firm doesn't mean you have to be cross. The ideal attitude is a balance of firmness with kindness.

THE MESSAGE OF FIRMNESS

Firmness is about managing behaviour and helping him feel safe. It is telling him 'I will help you make sense of the world' and 'There are some boundaries you must not cross and I care enough to defend those boundaries.'

THE MESSAGE OF KINDNESS

Kindness is about helping him to know at a very deep level 'You are accepted for exactly who you are' and 'You can never stop me loving you.' After there has been a problem, make a point of telling the child that you forgive him and that we all make mistakes and do things we shouldn't do from time to time. An important part of what a family is for is to be able to make mistakes and not have them held against us. Teach him that families are there to support each other.

Aim to speak to the child in a warm and kindly way even when you are saying 'no'. This will help *both* of you remember that you are still on his side even when you are being firm.

TIP # 56 Give feedback

Give him ongoing feedback on his behaviour to let him know how well he is doing. Try to give much more positive feedback than negative.

TIP # 57 Be flexible

Feel free to try out new ideas and strategies that you think of or come across, either in this book or anywhere else. If an idea works, and for as long as it works, go for it. Accept, reject, modify and adapt ideas to suit your unique situation. And don't forget that sometimes an idea that doesn't work today will work in six months time and vice versa.

TIP # 58 Think ahead

Be vigilant on behalf of the child, without being paranoid. Keep a lookout for potential 'booby traps', that is situations which are likely to cause major problems or anxiety for the child. Decide either to avoid such situations or have a plan of action to help him deal with them. Remember, prevention is better than cure and take steps to prevent problems before they arise.

TIP # 59 Present a united front

This can be hard to do, but if you can, try to make sure the relevant adults in the child's life agree on basic issues such as what the rules and standards are and how to handle problems. If you can present a united front, it lets the child know where he stands and prevents him from being able to play one adult off against the other.

TIP # 60 Choose your battles

It is impossible to tackle every single incident of poor behaviour that comes along and, even if it were possible, it would not be a good idea. If we are forever correcting and criticising a child, he can feel we are always on his back and just stop listening. This means he may not take us seriously if we ever need to talk to him about something really important. Also, continual battles can be exhausting, especially when you get into a head-to-head with a child on an issue that is impossible to enforce.

It is usually better to avoid confrontation than get into a battle and lose it, so sometimes it is better to turn a blind eye. However in the heat of the moment it's not always easy to decide whether an incident is worth tackling. Ask yourself two questions: first, how important is this really? second, is this a battle I might lose? (For example, you can't force a child to apologise but you can refuse to allow him to have a chocolate bar.) Remember, choose your battles carefully!

TIP # 61 Choose your timing

In some areas where your child's behaviour is very difficult or entrenched, it can be a huge challenge to help him to make any change. Only take on something like this when you are feeling very strong and on top of things. Bear in mind that when you tackle very entrenched behaviour it often gets worse before it gets better, so you may have to persevere through difficult times.

TIP # 62 Have a sense of humour

It's good to take our job as parents seriously of course, but sometimes it does us good just to lighten up!

Many of the antics of our AS children can be hilarious, especially at the times when they are being 'honest' and you don't want to hear it! Remember to laugh plenty and not to take things too seriously. The AS child needs to learn to laugh and have fun as well.

Encouraging Compliance and Motivation
Motivation absent

It can be very infuriating when a child seems to have no motivation or interest in conforming or doing a single thing you want him to do. But unfortunately this is a very common problem with AS children.

Most children are naturally motivated by the desire to compete with their peers or to please people in authority (or at least keep on the right side of them). But children with AS are often not that interested in pleasing others and the idea of competition is difficult for them (see Perfectionism, Tips 148–54). Given that such 'normal' motivation is largely absent in AS children, parents have to find other creative ways to influence their behaviour.

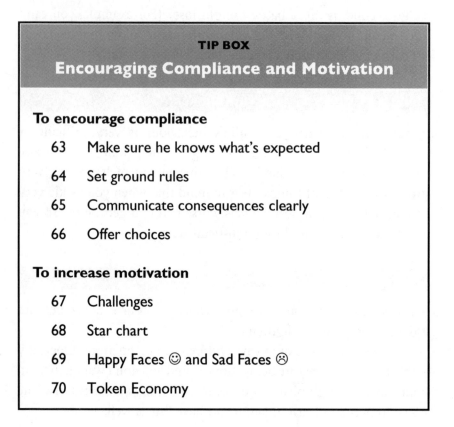

TIP BOX

Encouraging Compliance and Motivation

To encourage compliance

63   Make sure he knows what's expected

64   Set ground rules

65   Communicate consequences clearly

66   Offer choices

To increase motivation

67   Challenges

68   Star chart

69   Happy Faces ☺ and Sad Faces ☹

70   Token Economy

To encourage compliance

TIP # 63 Make sure he knows what's expected

When you are giving him instructions, make them as clear as possible. Give him SMART goals (see Tip 6). Remember he may need more guidance and reminders than you would expect. Do what you can to make sure he knows exactly what is expected of him. Write it down and, if need be, check he understands by having him repeat it back to you.

TIP # 64 Set ground rules

Set some basic ground rules. Make them simple, clear and easy to understand. Put them in writing and display them on the noticeboard (see Appendix 4).

TIP # 65 Communicate consequences clearly

Be very clear and consistent with the child about the consequences of his choices, whether good or bad. Make any sanctions or 'unfavourable consequences' realistic, fair and proportionate. Tell him the consequences calmly and carry them through consistently so he knows you mean what you say. Again, don't hint or leave any room for doubt. For example, say something very clear like, 'If you refuse to do your homework you will not be allowed to have pudding after your meal.'

And don't forget to tell him about favourable consequences too: for example, 'If you finish your homework you will have time to watch your video and you can have some chocolate pudding after tea.'

TIP # 66 Offer choices

If you sense a confrontation looming because the child is expected to do something he doesn't want to do, try to head it off by offering a choice rather than issuing an order or request. For instance, you could say, 'Would you like to come and do your homework right away or would you prefer to come in five minutes?' Of course he may reply defiantly, 'Neither. I don't want to do my homework at all.' If so, calmly make the situation clearer by saying something like, 'You must come. There is no choice on *whether* you do your homework. But you can have a choice on *when* you do it.'

It's not a bad idea, if he pushes it, to allow a bit of negotiation. This lets him see that you have taken his wishes into account. So you could compromise at say ten minutes and encourage him by saying something like, 'OK then I'll expect to see you back here in ten minutes. I hope you remember to come. But I'm sure you'll do your best to keep your word.' It may then be helpful to set a timer to beep after the agreed amount of time.

Here are some other examples of orders or requests being presented as choices:

- 'Would you prefer to put on your blue jacket or your red one?' – rather than 'Put on a jacket.'

- 'Would you like a large bowl of cereal or a small one?' – rather than 'You must have some cereal.'

To increase motivation

TIP # 67 Challenges

Make tasks interesting by presenting them as challenges that you are not sure he will be able to manage. For example: 'I wonder how long you can sit nicely at the table during teatime? I know it is quite hard for you to remember to sit still.' Don't get upset if he 'fails' the challenge but congratulate him if he manages it, even if he only has a small success. For instance: 'Well done, you stayed in your seat for five minutes.'

The following evening you could make the challenge a little harder: 'Remember you stayed at the table for five minutes last night. I wonder could you manage that two nights in a row?' or 'I suppose you would find it hard to stay for a longer time tonight?'

TIP # 68 Star chart

An ordinary star chart, such as is often used to help the behaviour of young children, can be effective even with an older AS child. Because of their visual appeal, star charts can help to encourage motivation and are quite easy either to buy or make.

TIP # 69 Happy Faces ☺ and Sad Faces ☹

Have a Happy Face ☺ and Sad Face ☹ notebook and award him Happy and Sad Faces depending on his behaviour during the day. This gives him visual feedback on how he is doing. Total up the score and use it as a basis for a reward or treat. Make sure he knows in advance what kind of behaviour will earn a Happy Face and what kind will earn a Sad Face. You could involve him in making out a list of some 'Happy Face behaviour' and some 'Sad Face behaviour' (see Appendix 8).

TIP # 70 Token Economy

This idea is a surefire winner that comes very directly from the principles of Applied Behaviour Analysis (ABA). There is a certain amount of work involved in setting it up, but it has the potential to get the child on side and turn behaviour around. It can be very useful if you have a major problem with compliance and motivation.

You will probably find you have to use the Token Economy for all your children because it will be so popular (see Appendices 2 and 3 for more information on ABA and the Token Economy).

Dealing with Difficult Moments

This section offers some suggestions on ways to deal with difficult situations such as embarrassing moments, stand-offs and arguments (see also Tips 78–87, Anger and Aggression).

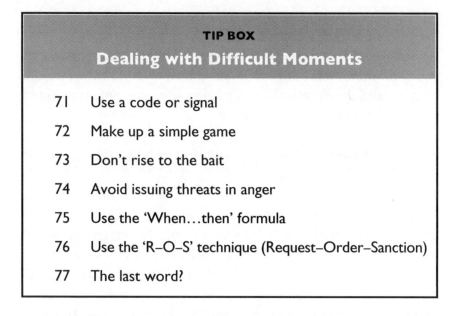

TIP BOX
Dealing with Difficult Moments

71   Use a code or signal

72   Make up a simple game

73   Don't rise to the bait

74   Avoid issuing threats in anger

75   Use the 'When...then' formula

76   Use the 'R–O–S' technique (Request–Order–Sanction)

77   The last word?

TIP # 71 Use a code or signal

This idea can be useful for when you are in company and want to tell the child something like: 'Be careful. Your behaviour is getting out of hand' without causing embarrassment. Have a special way of communicating behaviour warnings to your child by using special 'codes'. Codes could be, for example, pulling your earlobe, a special knock on a door or table, a special phrase or tap on the shoulder, or holding up a specific item such as a coloured card ('red cards' and 'yellow cards' may appeal to football fans). It can be fun coming up with the codes, although this needs to be done at the right moment, and they need to be in place and well established long before the difficult moment arises!

TIP # 72 Make up a simple game

When a stand-off or battle of wills has developed between you and the child and you are anticipating an explosion, sometimes making a simple game can defuse the situation. There are lots of possibilities and you will intuitively know what kind of thing is most likely to appeal to your child.

Here's one I remember using with my child. First I made sure I had his attention. Then I said to the other person in the room something like, 'Kenneth seems to be behaving badly and refusing to tidy up any of the toys he has thrown around the room... I wonder what would happen if I closed my eyes for 30 seconds... Let me just try it and see.'

I remember he was quite intrigued by this game and rushing around furiously tidying the toys while my eyes were closed. (I was of course 'amazed' and delighted at how well he had done while my eyes were closed!) This kind of approach can sometimes provide the child with a fun and face-saving way of backing down.

TIP # 73 Don't rise to the bait

Stay calm. Sometimes it seems as if the child is deliberately trying to provoke a confrontation. It is as if he needs to get a feeling of superiority or security by winning a confrontation. Make life easy for yourself by following two rules. First, avoid confrontation most of the time. Second, only get into confrontation when you are sure you can win!

TIP # 74 Avoid issuing threats in anger

Sometimes when you at the end of your tether it can be tempting to make wild threats. I'm sure we have all done this from time to time. We say crazy thing like: 'Right! That's it! I've had it! If you do that once more, this is the last time you will ever be allowed to go to the swimming pool!' Most children know we don't mean this and that we are only speaking in anger. But the AS child may take what we say literally. If so he might assume either that you are very mean, that you secretly hate him, or that you can't be relied upon to be honest (because of course he does go to the swimming pool again).

TIP # 75 The 'When...then' formula

When he is getting out of line, keep your voice level and use the 'When...then' formula. For example, use the wording: '*When* you stop shouting, *then* I will answer your question.' It is important to say 'when' rather than 'if'.

Repeat it like a broken record, if need be, and don't allow yourself to be drawn into an argument.

TIP # 76 Use the 'R-O-S' technique (Request–Order–Sanction)

This is a useful tactic for when you come up against *deliberate disobediance and defiance.*

- First make the *request*: e.g. 'Will you please stop swinging on the curtains?'

- Then make it into an *order*. Say, for instance, 'I have asked you nicely. Now I am ordering you.' Or even, 'This is no longer a request. It is an order.'

- Finally issue an appropriate *sanction.*

TIP # 77 The last word?

When an argument or a battle of wills develops, sometimes the AS child tries to drag the dialogue on and on, just so he can have the final word. Try not to let yourself be drawn into a prolonged dispute, but if there is an issue that you think is important, be consistent about your stance.

Take, for example, a case where the child 'insists' that you must make his bed and you 'insist' that he must make it. Accept that you don't have the power to *force* him to make the bed and that it may end up unmade that day. But you do have the power to remove a privilege such as time on the computer. Don't get into an lengthy argument. State expectations and consequences calmly and clearly and stick to them. **Keep in mind that the important thing is to have the *lasting* word rather than the *last* word.**

3

Common Problems

A–Z

Anger and Aggression

A quick overview of the problem

Angry outbursts in a child with Asperger Syndrome can seem:

- extreme
- immature
- unpredictable
- unreasonable
- out of control.

What this can lead to:

- Parents and teachers find him hard to manage.
- They end up becoming frustrated, drained and exhausted.
- The child becomes increasingly unpopular.

Asperger extremes

Children with Asperger Syndrome have difficulties on a daily basis with many things that other children take for granted and at times this must cause them overwhelming anxiety and frustration. It is inevitable that these feelings will sometimes spill over and be expressed as rage or aggression.

Yet according to the experts, an AS child can be at either end of two extremes – he can either be extremely prone to anger or else extremely docile. An angry AS child might fly off into a rage following what looks like very little provocation. At the other extreme, a docile AS child can seem almost devoid of anger, no matter what the provocation. Sometimes the same child will display both of these extremes on different days or in different situations.

The short-term and longer term strategies

The AS child needs to learn how to recognise and understand anger in himself and others, as well as how to control it. The last thing we want is for him to get used to anger and aggression as his means of dealing with his difficulties. We can't afford to turn a blind eye. Physical violence especially is a serious issue and can even be dangerous.

To tackle problems with out-of-control anger and aggression, you really need to have two strategies. First, you need a short-term strategy to help you handle explosive situations as and when they arise. Second, you need a longer term strategy to help you gradually train the child, so that hopefully in the end such situations no longer happen. The tips in this section are designed to help you deal with explosive situations as they arise – or even better, to prevent them before they happen, where possible.

TIP BOX

Anger and Aggression

78   Take action at an early age

79   Show him safe ways to express and manage his anger

80   Take steps to avert a crisis

81   Reward him for keeping his cool

82   'Zany expletives'

Ideas for dealing with a crisis (see also Tips 71–7, Dealing with Difficult Moments)

83   Have a Crisis Plan

84   Nip explosive situations in the bud

85   Stay calm

86   Don't give in to intimidation

87   Let him play to an empty stage

TIP # 78 Take action at an early age

There are several reasons for tackling problems involving anger and aggression when the child is as young as possible:

- He is easier to deal with while he is still smaller than you!

- The longer the behaviour continues, the more the pattern becomes established and the harder it is to break.

- The child may come to see aggression as his way of expressing himself or getting his own way.

- He may get to enjoy the feeling of control he gets from this kind of behaviour because it serves as a kind of substitute for the feelings of acceptance and security he really needs.

- If he gets a bad reputation it may become self-fulfilling and cause problems in school and elsewhere. People may not welcome his company and as a result he may become isolated and alienated. If this goes on into adulthood, it has the potential to create huge problems, both for him and for the people around him.

TIP # 79 Show him safe ways to express and manage his anger

Look out for good moments when he is already calm and talk to him about anger. Reassure him that everybody feels angry sometimes and that's OK. Remind him that the problem is not angry *feelings* but some angry *behaviour*. Discuss with him some alternative ways of expressing his anger which are not destructive, and make a list of 'Anger Dos and Don'ts' (see Appendix 6). Then when you see the warning signs, you can remind him of his alternatives.

TIP # 80 Take steps to avert a crisis

Remember – prevention is better than cure. It is not always possible to avoid a crisis but there are steps you can take to set things up so they do not get out of hand too often. Many of these are outlined in other sections. For example:

- Use a code or signal (see Tip 71).
- Offer choices (see Tip 66).
- Nip explosive situations in the bud (see Tip 84).
- Use a timer or stopwatch (see Tip 29).
- Make up a simple game (see Tip 72).

TIP# 81 Reward him for keeping his cool

Make 'keeping your cool' a specific goal. When you see him keeping his cool in a situation that you know he finds difficult, acknowledge it and praise him for it, even if it's only a small thing. For example, say something like: 'I noticed you really kept your cool when your baby brother upset your Lego display. You must have felt very disappointed when that happened. But you did well to stay quite calm. I'm really proud of you. That shows a lot of self-control. Well done!'

TIP # 82 'Zany expletives'

If the child is using expletives, let him think up some of his own originals as substitutes. It is not nearly as offensive. A common example of this is when people say 'Sugar!' rather than another four-letter word which also begins with the 'sh' sound! The more zany the expletive, the better.

Try something like 'Shhhhhogglemidoozlum!' to get you started. It can be fun thinking up your own long and expressive swear words – and 'zany expletives' are much less likely to get you into trouble!

Ideas for dealing with a crisis

TIP# 83 Have a Crisis Plan

It can be very difficult to deal with a crisis in the heat of the moment. How do you manage to control the child's anger as well as perhaps your own? Step back and look at the strategies you use to deal with crisis situations at present. It might help if you write them down. Assess them realistically. What has worked? What hasn't? Are there any new ideas that might be worth a try? You are best placed to know what is most likely to work for your child.

From that work out your own Crisis Plan. This will help you and your child know in advance exactly what steps you are going to take if an 'explosion' occurs.

Try out your Crisis Plan and monitor how it works. If need be, adapt it and try new ideas as you go along.

TIP # 84 Nip explosive situations in the bud

When you see an explosive situation developing, don't let it get too far out of hand before you step in.

TIP # 85 Stay calm

When things are getting heated, don't add fuel to the fire. Use a calm, unemotional tone of voice. Try not to panic or to issue threats in anger.

TIP # 86 Don't give in to intimidation

Try not to give in or let the child have his own way when he badgers you or becomes aggressive or intimidating. Give him the impression that his poor behaviour makes it *less* likely that he will get his way, not more. For example, try saying something like: 'I realise you want those chocolates and you want them right now. But at the moment I don't allow you to have them and I'm not prepared even to *discuss* it with you because of how you're behaving. When you have calmed down, then we can talk about possibly having some later.' (Note: Use the 'When ...then' formula.)

TIP # 87 Let him play to an empty stage

If the child becomes violent, consider removing yourself and other people from room if the situation warrants it. Sometimes removing the audience can help take the heat out of the situation.

Attention Difficulties

A quick overview of the problem

The AS child may have difficulties in the following areas:

- concentrating
- paying attention
- organisation
- keeping/sitting still.

What this can lead to:

- He has difficulty doing some things that require him to settle down and sit still, such as staying at the table for a meal.
- He seems to be forever on the move, for example, climbing excessively and inappropriately.
- His performance at school may be affected.

Asperger extremes

When it comes to important skills such as concentration, paying attention and applying himself, the AS child can be full of contradictions. Sometimes he goes into a kind of 'hyperfocus'; for example, spending hours absorbed obsessively in his special interest or activity, or on his favourite computer game. Other times he seems to be hardly capable of focusing or paying attention at all. As with many Asperger traits, there are extremes but very little 'happy medium'.

Assessing the problem

If the child has attention difficulties, first of all they need to be recognised for what they are. Depending on the degree of the difficulties, you may suspect that your child has Attention Deficit Disorder (ADD).

If so, a qualified expert will be able to assess your child properly for you. However, no matter what the diagnosis, it is important to accept the genuineness of his difficulties. A realistic attitude puts you in a better position to help him and can prevent a lot of frustration all round.

THE WIDER IMPLICATIONS

Attention difficulties can cause a lot of problems for the child, especially if they are not recognised and understood. It is very easy for his behaviour to be misinterpreted. At school he may well underperform and be considered less bright than he really is, or he can seem lazy and unco-operative. Difficulties with concentration may cause some of the following problems:

- His teacher finds it hard to get him to stay at his desk.
- He doesn't concentrate on his work very well.
- His attention wanders a lot.
- He daydreams.
- He can be forgetful and absent-minded.

Difficulties with organisation skills may mean:

- He is meticulously tidy or alternatively he is the complete opposite. Either way, he is intolerant of any interference with his way of doing things.
- If he is asked to do something, he genuinely intends to do it, but then forgets what he is supposed to be doing.

Restlessness may mean:

- He is very fidgety and finds it hard to stay still.
- It's very hard to get him to sit in one place, for example, to have a meal or do his homework.
- He is forever climbing and clambering round the furniture, for example.

Tackling the problems

Ultimately we want the AS child to get to the stage where he can manage his own life in a way that is orderly but not obsessive. A key strategy for doing this is to provide him with the very clear structure that he needs. This will help him know where he stands and what is expected of him.

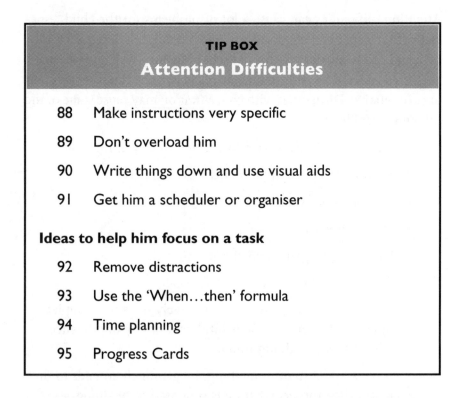

TIP BOX

Attention Difficulties

88   Make instructions very specific

89   Don't overload him

90   Write things down and use visual aids

91   Get him a scheduler or organiser

Ideas to help him focus on a task

92   Remove distractions

93   Use the 'When…then' formula

94   Time planning

95   Progress Cards

TIP # 88 Make instructions very specific

Make sure the child understands very clearly what is expected. Make instructions brief and to the point (see also Tip 53, Communicate clearly). Give him SMART goals (see Tip 6).

TIP # 89 Don't overload him

Don't overload him with a lot of information or instructions and don't give him too many things to do at once, because he may find that very hard to process. For example, instead of giving him a series of tasks, just give him one at a time to do, or break tasks into several different steps and praise and reward him for each one. (See Appendix 9, for an example of how to break showering into smaller steps.)

TIP # 90 Write things down and use visual aids

Some visual aids can help him to organise himself:

- An ordinary calendar, to let him see what the plans are for the coming week or the month.

- A timetable. This can be either a daily or weekly timetable. It is very easy to make your own timetable by ruling a sheet of paper into the appropriate sections for the day or week as needed. If you laminate it, then it can be used again and again.

- Reminders or lists (see also Tips 30 and 31).

TIP # 91 Get him a scheduler or organiser

Even if he is quite young, you could help him use his own organiser book. These are easily available and there are plenty to choose from which are designed to appeal to children. He might feel quite important using the memos, reminders and dayplanners, etc. If he is older, or interested in gadgets, he might even enjoy an electronic organiser. Using such devices can be good training for future life, when they may well prove invaluable.

Ideas to help him focus on a task

TIP # 92 Remove distractions

To help him focus on a task, keep distractions to an absolute minimum. This may mean turning off the TV and phone for half an hour. It may also mean making the area where he is working clutter-free. If he has a task to do at the table, clear it of everything except what is strictly needed for the task.

TIP # 93 Use the 'When ... then' formula

To keep his attention focused on a task, use the 'When...then' formula. For example: '*When* you have finished tidying your toys away, *then* you can watch TV.'

TIP # 94 Time planning

If it is difficult to get him to settle down to a specific task, write down what you want him to do and for how long. If neccessary, negotiate a time with him. This can be done very simply, for example:

Homework: 20 minutes

Then

Playstation: 30 minutes

You could set a timer or alarm clock to go off after the agreed time. (If he stops before the 20 minutes homework has been done, start the timer again!)

TIP # 95 Progress Cards

If he has difficulty with performing a series of tasks, make a 'Progress Card'. The idea is to set out the tasks very clearly so he can see what needs to be done as well as the order in which they are to be done. Then when they are ticked off, he can see they are done. For example:

✓ Go upstairs

✓ Get undressed

✓ Put on pyjamas

✓ Put clothes away

✓ Come down for supper

Bedtime and Sleeping

A quick overview of the problem

- The child is very difficult to settle at night and sleeps poorly.

What this can lead to:

- The following day he is tired, cross and harder than usual to manage.

- Other members of the family also become tired and cross.

- Performance at school and work suffers.

Impact on the family

When a child has problems settling at night it can be hard on the whole family, especially if he won't stay in his room and keeps demanding attention well after bedtime. A lot of AS children seem to be poor sleepers. My own son is one of them. It's not unusual to find him still awake well after midnight. (Sometimes I think he needs less sleep than I do!)

The adults in the family get worn out and exhausted if they don't get the break they need in the evening. Other children in the family also need their sleep and may find it hard to settle while they know their AS brother is still wide awake and refusing to settle. They may decide to follow his example by refusing to stay in bed as well, because they feel it is unfair that he is being allowed to 'get away with it'. Everybody can end up tired and grumpy the next day, and find it harder to cope. Performance at school and work suffers. The following evening the parents may be too tired to take steps to try and turn things around and so a vicious cycle develops.

As parents we worry when a child doesn't sleep well. Sometimes we wonder whether a decent night's sleep might be just what he needs to help his mood and his behaviour. We know our children need plenty of sleep and we feel it's our job to make sure they get enough.

Tackling the problems

It may be that the child genuinely doesn't need as much sleep as you think. At any rate, it is impossible to *make* a child go to asleep. The best we can do is make the conditions favourable so as to encourage him to get the rest he needs.

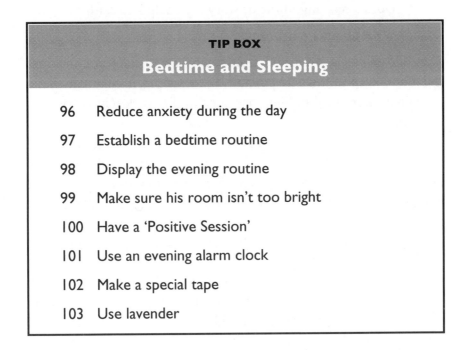

TIP BOX

Bedtime and Sleeping

96	Reduce anxiety during the day
97	Establish a bedtime routine
98	Display the evening routine
99	Make sure his room isn't too bright
100	Have a 'Positive Session'
101	Use an evening alarm clock
102	Make a special tape
103	Use lavender

TIP # 96 Reduce anxiety during the day

If the child has been uptight and anxious all day, this will make it harder for him to get to sleep. So in a way we can start tackling bedtime and sleeping problems long before evening comes by taking steps to reduce anxiety (for ideas on reducing anxiety, see Tips 24–34).

TIP # 97 Establish a bedtime routine

Aim to have a calm, predictable routine at bedtime, which may mean establishing some reassuring rituals. Think about what helps him feel secure and relaxed, so you can incorporate it into his routine, for example:

- Does he have favourite pyjamas, quilt or sleeping bag?
- Does he like a warm milky drink?
- Is he better with one favourite cuddly toy or with several?
- Does he like to be read a story?
- Does a relaxing music or story tape help him settle?
- What about a quiet chat?

The child gains a lot of security from having a predictable routine. So it is good to keep to it where possible. For example, if he usually has a ten-minute story read to him, then stick to this as closely as you can. Use a timer if necessary.

On the other hand it is impossible always to have things completely predictable. Unforeseen events do come along. And anyway it's not a good idea to encourage him to become too hung up on exact timings. So aim for a balance between predictability and flexibility.

TIP # 98 Display the evening routine

Work out an evening routine that is realistic and manageable. Make sure the child knows exactly what to expect by displaying it on the noticeboard. A simple example would be:

Jim's Evening Routine

Supper: 7.00

Bathroom and pyjamas on: 7.30

Storytime: 7.45

Lights off: 8.15

TIP # 99 Make sure his room isn't too bright

Unless they are afraid of the dark, most children sleep better if the bedroom is dark after 'light off' time. They often find it harder to sleep during the brighter summer nights. Check whether the curtains or blinds are keeping out the light properly. Heavier curtains or a lightproof blind (sometimes known as a blackout blind) may help to make the room more conducive to rest and sleep.

TIP # 100 Have a 'Positive Session'

Sometimes it is reassuring and fun in the evening to have a 'Positive Session' when you talk over the events of the day (see Tip 21).

TIP # 101 Use an evening alarm clock

Set an alarm clock in his bedroom for 'light off' time, which goes off at the same time every night. This may seem like a strange idea, but it can help to establish a very definite and unarguable end to the day.

TIP # 102 Make a special tape

Read a special story or sing a song onto a tape for him. This could be useful for any evenings when you are not available to do it in person.

TIP # 103 Use lavender

Lavender is supposed to be a calming fragrance. Try putting some in his room. It can be burned on an aromatherapy burner, or a lavender sachet can be placed under his pillow.

Depression

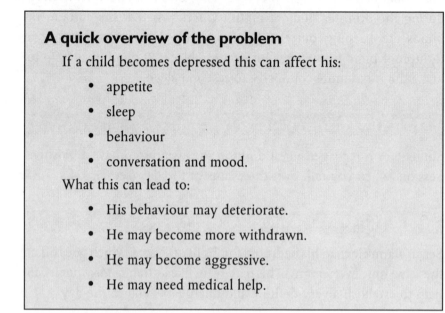

A quick overview of the problem

If a child becomes depressed this can affect his:

- appetite
- sleep
- behaviour
- conversation and mood.

What this can lead to:

- His behaviour may deteriorate.
- He may become more withdrawn.
- He may become aggressive.
- He may need medical help.

Depression and Asperger Syndrome

The experts tell us that an adult with Asperger Syndrome has an increased risk of depression and it is not hard to understand why. A major reason must be the social difficulties.

Whether he admits it or not, an AS person wants to have friends and feel accepted, but the world can seem a frustrating, unpredictable and confusing place to him. School for the AS child, which is a big part of any child's life, is a 'social minefield'. He just doesn't know quite how to be accepted and to 'succeed'.

It is important for us to be aware of the risk of depression without becoming paranoid. Our basic goal is to help him to be happy with who he is and to accept his Asperger Syndrome as part of himself.

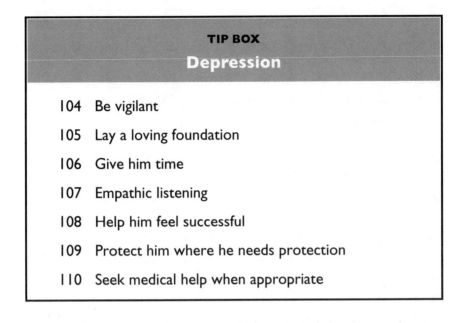

TIP BOX

Depression

104 Be vigilant

105 Lay a loving foundation

106 Give him time

107 Empathic listening

108 Help him feel successful

109 Protect him where he needs protection

110 Seek medical help when appropriate

TIP # 104 Be vigilant

Be aware that depression is a risk for people with Asperger Syndrome. So without being overconcerned or paranoid, keep a lookout for signs and symptoms of depression developing. If a child is unhappy or depressed this may manifest in any of the following ways:

- insomnia
- anxiety
- aggression
- moodiness and bad temper
- being quiet and withdrawn.

TIP # 105 Lay a loving foundation

It is impossible to guarantee that depression will not develop of course, but we can at least lay a foundation that makes the conditions as favourable as possible for him (see Chapter 1).

TIP # 106 Give him time

Spend some time together one-to-one if you can, doing something quiet and relaxing. Take him for an easygoing walk, perhaps along the shore or on a nature ramble. Have fun doing simple things like gathering up shells or coloured stones.

TIP # 107 Empathic listening

Often when an AS child is upset or depressed, he gets things way out of proportion and his thinking can become rigid and unreasonable. As parents, we find it very hard to sit by and watch this happen, because naturally we hate to see him upset. We feel like trying to 'fix' things for him and make him feel better. Some of the ways in which we try to 'fix' things when he is upset or depressed are by:

- consoling him that things are not that bad
- providing a solution to his problem
- trying to make him 'see sense' and get things into proportion.

And of course all of these ideas can be good at times, but they are not always helpful, especially when the child is upset over something that seems bizarre or unreasonable. We need to accept that no matter how hard we find it to understand, the way he sees it is the way he sees it. His upset feelings are very real and it can be counter-productive to try and fix things for him at the 'wrong' time, that is, while he is still upset. If you do, he can get the impression that you are trivialising his concerns and you just don't understand. This can make him more entrenched, hostile or withdrawn.

But the wrong moment for 'fixing' things can also be the right moment to build some trust in the relationship between the two of you. Because sometimes when he is upset, what he needs from you most is not that you 'fix' things but that you show him you are on his side by providing a sympathetic listening ear.

Listen to his grievances in an interested, accepting, non-judgemental way. Let him talk as much or as little as he wants to. Just sound sympathetic and on his side and resist the urge to 'fix'. Don't interrupt too much, but if he seems to need a reply, try and restrict your comments to general sympathetic remarks like: 'That's too bad' or 'I'm sorry to hear you're having such a rough time.'

TIP # 108 Help him feel successful

If he is going through a rough time, take the pressure off where you can. When making plans, assess whether it is likely to be a positive experience for him. Don't stretch him too much to do things he finds difficult because it may undermine his confidence and make him feel like a failure.

Look for ways to give him little experiences of success. Let him focus his attention on things he is good at for the time being, whether it be playing a computer game or drawing pictures. Look for opportunities to congratulate him upon his efforts, achievements and positive attributes.

TIP # 109 Protect him where he needs protection

All sorts of situations can cause anxiety for the child with Asperger Syndrome, especially social situations. He needs us to protect him without overprotecting him and this can be a difficult balance to achieve. As parents, there are times when we need to recognise his vulnerability and protect him from situations which provoke more anxiety than he can cope with. This may mean, for example, that at certain times we need to make the judgement that he needs a period of time off school. (If he is having problems at school or being bullied, see Tips 166–68.)

TIP # 110 Seek medical help when appropriate

If you are concerned about your child's mood or suspect that he may be becoming clinically depressed, seek medical help.

Food Issues

A quick overview of the problem

Many children with Asperger Syndrome are fussy and obsessive to some extent about their diet. For example, the typical AS child may:

- be faddy and obsessive about what he will eat and drink
- consume from a very restricted range of foods
- generally consume extremely small quantities
- consume extremely large quantities.

What this can lead to:

- His health and size may be affected.
- Parents become anxious and distressed.
- Other people judge that he is being spoiled.

Understanding the problem

A lot of children don't eat well but in the case of children with AS the difficulties can be much more extreme than normal childhood faddiness. It can be a very worrying, frustrating problem. And hard to remedy, because of course it is impossible to *make* a child eat sensibly.

Food is essential for life and a source of great pleasure to most people, so it is hard to understand this difficulty. Some of the main reasons would seem to involve:

- anxiety, aggravated by an extreme sensation of disgust
- sensory issues
- control issues.

ANXIETY AND DISGUST

My son has extreme difficulties with food and he feels that people do not understand how difficult eating is for him. Yet he finds it very hard to explain why. The thing he hates most is trying something new or unfamiliar. Sometimes when I have watched him try to do this, the expression on his face has looked something like extreme disgust combined with fear or anxiety.

Perhaps the best way for us to understand how the 'fussy' AS child feels is to think of something we find utterly disgusting and then imagine how we would feel if someone tried to force us to eat it.

SENSORY ISSUES

Eating problems can be aggravated by sensory difficulties. The child may suffer aversions to certain tastes, colours or textures. There may also be obsessional preferences for certain foods. Pringles crisps are quite a common favourite, presumably because of their consistent, predictable shape and texture, as well as their distinctive taste.

CONTROL ISSUES

Another factor that can creep into dietary management is the issue of control. Psychologists tell us that food is one of the first areas where a young child can experience control in his life. He discovers at an early stage that he has the power to accept or reject food. If he gets to enjoy that feeling of power, he can come to see food rejection as a way of having the control he craves, especially over the adults in his life! And of course this is more likely to happen when we make too much of an issue of food.

How parents might feel

Eating problems can be a great worry and especially hard for a mum to cope with. Feeding her child is a natural part of mothering and when a child refuses food she ends up feeling powerless, inadequate and rejected. The constant friction and frustrations can make it harder for her to manage the problem in a loving and effective way.

Additionally, eating out with the AS child can be extremely difficult, not only because of his eating quirks, but also because of his social and behavioural difficulties. When other people witness his eating habits and behaviour, you may well get looks of disapproval from people who imagine you are spoiling and pandering to him. It can be a very embarrassing experience. (At such times remember Tip 11: *'Those who mind don't matter and those who matter don't mind!'*)

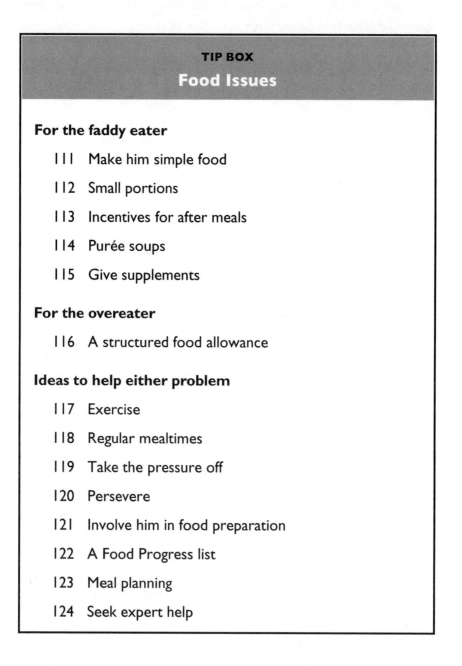

TIP BOX
Food Issues

For the faddy eater

- 111   Make him simple food
- 112   Small portions
- 113   Incentives for after meals
- 114   Purée soups
- 115   Give supplements

For the overeater

- 116   A structured food allowance

Ideas to help either problem

- 117   Exercise
- 118   Regular mealtimes
- 119   Take the pressure off
- 120   Persevere
- 121   Involve him in food preparation
- 122   A Food Progress list
- 123   Meal planning
- 124   Seek expert help

For the faddy eater

TIP # 111 Make him simple food

When you go to a lot of trouble preparing food and then the child refuses to eat it, it is hard not to get upset and cross with him. And getting cross with him usually does no good at all.

If you offer him simple food that takes little effort to prepare, this can take a lot of pressure off all round. (Bananas and milk are some of the original 'fast foods'!)

TIP # 112 Small portions

When you are trying to introduce new foods, offer small portions and build up the amounts very gradually. Reward him for trying even a tiny amount.

TIP # 113 Incentives for after meals

A FOOD TREAT AS AN INCENTIVE

Offer a treat that you know he will enjoy as an incentive for him to eat up his meal. As well as telling him about it so he can look forward to it, set it out so that he can actually see it. Use the 'When...then' formula, for example, '*When* you have finished your fish fingers, *then* you can have your slice of cake.'

A FUN ACTIVITY AS AN INCENTIVE

Schedule activities that he enjoys for straight after the meal: '*When* you have finished your meal, *then* you can play with your new jigsaw.'

TIP # 114 Purée soups

Puréed soups are good for hiding vegetables or other nutritious ingredients and can help get around the problem of the child who hates 'bits'. If you can find a basic stock flavour that he likes, you can sneak in nourishing extras and liquidise it all together!

TIP # 115 Give supplements

If you are concerned about whether he is getting enough nutrients, it could be worth giving him some nutritional supplements. A doctor or dietician can give advice on what nutrients he is missing. Supplements are available in various different forms and if your child is reluctant to take tablets you could try, for example, drops, capsules, medicine, or fruity drinks.

For the overeater

TIP # 116 A structured food allowance

Make a list of the foods that he is eating and divide them into food groups (fruit and vegetables, protein, and so on) so that you and he can *see* where his diet is out of balance. Ascertain what food group he is eating too much of and make that group the 'rationed' group. For example, if he has too many cakes and chocolate bars, set a strict daily allowance of those that he can ration out over the course of the day. Display the daily allowance on the noticeboard and let him cross it off each day to indicate when he has had his allowance.

Ideas to help either problem

TIP # 117 Exercise

Exercise can help balance the effects of overeating or undereating and serve as a distraction from food. Try to encourage plenty of exercise and not too many snacks and drinks between meals. This will encourage the child to develop a healthy appetite.

TIP # 118 Regular mealtimes

Give him a clear familiar routine by making mealtimes as regular as you can. Try to encourage him to come to the table, even if it is only for a small part of the mealtime and he just eats a little. Regular mealtimes might also reduce snacking if the child knows when to expect the next meal.

TIP # 119 Take the pressure off

Ideally, mealtimes should be relaxing, enjoyable occasions, not battlegrounds! Try and avoid battles by making food less of an issue. It is an extremely hard thing to do but try not to show it, even when you *are* anxious and upset.

TIP # 120 Persevere

You can't force him to eat but you can keep on offering him the food you want him to eat. For example, if you would like him to have some bread at teatime, rather than making a fuss keep putting some on the table every evening beside his meal. (Eventually one evening he might have a try!)

TIP # 121 Involve him in food preparation

Occasionally let him help choose a healthy, tasty meal, or bake something from a recipe book. Keep it realistic and not too ambitious. Prepare a shopping list and go shopping for the ingredients together. Then let him feel involved in the cooking by taking part in some aspect of it that he would enjoy, such as stirring, whipping cream or sprinkling chocolate drops.

TIP # 122 A Food Progress list

Keep a list on the noticeboard of all the foods he eats and add to the list as he tries new ones. Praise and reward him for any healthy additions.

TIP # 123 Meal planning

Avoid the hassle of endless and frustrating arguments about what he will or won't eat every mealtime, by letting him choose in advance. Make out a Meal List at the beginning of the week and display it on the noticeboard.

TIP # 124 Seek expert help

If you do seek medical help, keep a record of a typical week's consumption to bring along to the appointment. Include all food and drinks together with amounts. Your doctor may refer you to a dietician who will be able to tell you where the deficiencies are and give advice.

Handwriting

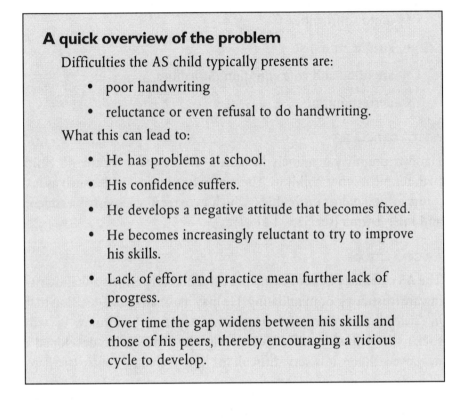

A quick overview of the problem

Difficulties the AS child typically presents are:

- poor handwriting
- reluctance or even refusal to do handwriting.

What this can lead to:

- He has problems at school.
- His confidence suffers.
- He develops a negative attitude that becomes fixed.
- He becomes increasingly reluctant to try to improve his skills.
- Lack of effort and practice mean further lack of progress.
- Over time the gap widens between his skills and those of his peers, thereby encouraging a vicious cycle to develop.

'I hate handwriting'

A lot of AS children seem to hate handwriting and will do all they can to avoid it. It can develop into quite a battle and lead to a lot of frustration for all concerned. It is hard to know how wise it is for parents to get involved in this issue. Some may prefer to leave the battle to the school because they don't want to risk putting the child off even more by keeping it going at home. And anyway there are always plenty of other important issues to keep them busy!

On the other hand it is hard to avoid becoming involved completely, especially when there is homework to be done, or when it is clear that handwriting difficulties are affecting his overall confidence. (See also Motor Skills and Co-ordination, Tips 141–7).

Why do they hate handwriting?

Here are some of the main factors which may cause or contribute to the child's difficulties:

- motor difficulties
- a rigid attitude
- attention and concentration difficulties
- perfectionism.

MOTOR DIFFICULTIES

Handwriting may genuinely be a more difficult task for the AS child than for most other children. There may be physical issues such as lax joints or fine motor difficulties, which may require expert assessment and intervention (see Tips 141–7).

A RIGID ATTITUDE

The AS child may be very easily put off if his early efforts at handwriting are frustrating or humiliating. He may make an initial decision that he 'hates' handwriting. Because of his Asperger Syndrome, he will stick to this attitude with an extreme rigidity. Once he has developed a negative attitude, it is very difficult for him to change course (see Tips 155–8).

ATTENTION AND CONCENTRATION DIFFICULTIES

It is very hard to concentrate on something that you absolutely hate doing (see Tips 88–95).

PERFECTIONISM

The AS child hates to feel criticised and so from his point of view there is good reason to avoid handwriting if he does not feel he is good at it. He may be very disappointed in his early efforts because they look shakey and wobbly. One little AS girl became very upset when she was learning to write because she expected her writing to look immediately exactly like the teacher's writing.

Additionally, the idea of expressing himself in writing may be offputting to an AS child. Handwriting leaves him open to feelings of failure and criticism, not only of his letter formation but also of what he might reveal of himself through his writing (see Tips 148–54).

Tackling the problem

The only way to improve any skill is through practice. But how do you get a reluctant child to co-operate in an activity when he has a negative attitude and can't see the point? The problem is that if you keep nagging at him, you can end up just putting him off even more. The key is to find ways to increase his motivation.

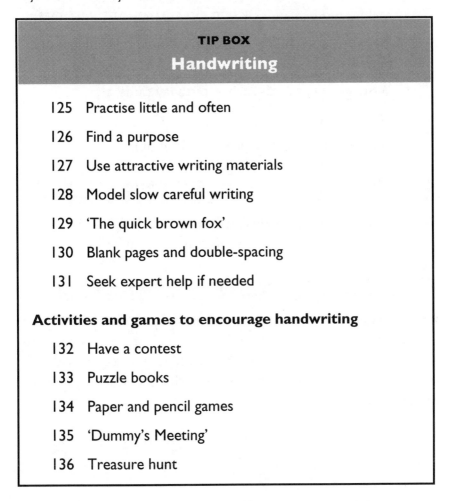

TIP BOX
Handwriting

125 Practise little and often

126 Find a purpose

127 Use attractive writing materials

128 Model slow careful writing

129 'The quick brown fox'

130 Blank pages and double-spacing

131 Seek expert help if needed

Activities and games to encourage handwriting

132 Have a contest

133 Puzzle books

134 Paper and pencil games

135 'Dummy's Meeting'

136 Treasure hunt

TIP # 125 Practise little and often

Long, arduous handwriting sessions are likely to put him off. Be flexible and err on the side of more frequent, shorter sessions. Stop the session on a positive note before he gets too restless and congratulate him on how well he has done. A five-minute session that is positive and fun is better in the long run than a 15-minute battle.

TIP # 126 Find a purpose

If there is a purpose which interests him, this might help overcome his reluctance, for example:

- Make a door sign (e.g. KEEP OUT: MICHAEL'S ROOM).
- Write a list pertaining to his special interest (e.g. types of butterfly).
- Write greetings cards such as birthday cards, etc.
- Start a diary.
- Write a letter (e.g. to a penpal or relation).

TIP # 127 Use attractive writing materials

For example, if he dislikes pencil, try crayon or felt tip. But be careful not to offer too large a choice, as this may prove to be a distraction.

TIP # 128 Model slow careful writing

It is not helpful for him to see you dashing off your own handwriting in a way that seems effortless or careless. Even if you are only writing a cheque to pay a bill, let him see you take a little moment extra with it. It is a good example to him if he sees you taking a pride in your own handwriting.

TIP # 129 'The quick brown fox'

'The quick brown fox jumped over the lazy dog.' This sentence uses every letter in the alphabet, which makes it useful as a basis for practicework or writing contests.

TIP # 130 Blank pages and double-spacing

If the child has a lengthy piece of prose such as a story to write for homework, he may find it easier to write on alternate pages and use alternate lines. This makes it easier later on to do the correction and expansion work that he dislikes.

TIP # 131 Seek expert help if needed

If you suspect that your child has any kind of physical problem such as poor hand–eye co-ordination or lax joints, seek expert help. An occupational therapist can make an assessment and give advice and recommendations.

Activities and games which encourage handwriting

TIP # 132 Have a contest

For example: How neat can I make a letter A? How many neat and properly formed letter Ms can I form in 30 seconds?

TIP # 133 Puzzle books

There are lots of great puzzle books available for children, that contain pencil and paper activities which he might enjoy, for example:

- dot-to-dot puzzles
- mazes
- colouring pictures

- word searches
- crossword puzzles.

If you can find one based on your child's special interest or favourite cartoon character, it could be very helpful. Even if he is not actually writing, at least if he enjoys them they could help overcome his reluctance to use a pencil or pen.

It is also quite easy to prepare and laminate your own reusable dot-to-dots of the letters of the alphabet, or of the child's name, or whatever you want him to practise. As the child makes progress, the dots can then be drawn closer together.

TIP # 134 Paper and pencil games

Have fun playing games like Hangman, Battleships or Noughts and Crosses.

TIP # 135 'Dummy's Meeting'

Have a fun game of 'Dummy's Meeting' where everyone is allowed to write messages to each other in a notebook, but no one is allowed to speak.

TIP # 136 Treasure hunt

The hider hides a small 'treasure' and leaves a series of written clues to help the hunter or hunters find it. Each clue either sets a 'task' or gives directions to the next clue, until the prize is found. It can be played either in teams or individually. Players take turns at being 'hider', although they may need an adult on their team.

Homework Supervision

A quick overview of the problem

Whether you are homeschooling your child or simply trying to get him to do his homework, the difficulties tend to be the same. Getting the AS child to co-operate can be a very hard job!
What this can lead to:

- frustration at home

- problems in school

- his academic performance and progress suffer.

Tackling the problems

The key strategies needed to help the child with homework difficulties are to give him the help he needs in the areas of:

- handwriting difficulties (see Tips 125–36)

- attention and organisation difficulties (see Tips 88–95)

- providing him with the structure that he needs.

TIP BOX
Homework Supervision

Providing structure

137 Prepare

138 Take charge

139 Provide a very structured setting

140 Use the 'When…then' formula

Prepare

TIP # 137 Prepare

Prepare a simple Work Planner. Have everything that you need organised beforehand, including stopwatch and timer if appropriate. For example:

> Work Planner
> ✓ Reading: pages 3–6
> ✓ Maths problem 5
> ✓ Maths problem 6
> ✓ Maths problem 7

TIP # 138 Take charge

Use a friendly but firm manner to make sure he knows you are in charge.

TIP # 139 Provide a very structured setting

Do the work in an environment where there are no distractions, like books, toys or TV. Show him the Work Planner and tell him a few minutes or so in advance that work will be starting in x minutes. Let him cross off the items on the Work Planner, or else see you cross them off, when they are complete.

TIP # 140 Use the 'When...then' formula

If he seems non-compliant, appear unemotional but try using the 'When...then' formula: e.g. '*When* you have finished this piece of work, *then* you will have your supper.'

Motor Skills and Co-ordination

A quick overview of the problem

The child may suffer from some degree of difficulty with:

- fine motor skills – (he may lack dexterity)
- gross motor skills – (he may be somewhat clumsy).

This may lead to struggles with a lot of important childhood skills such as:

- using a knife and fork
- tying shoelaces
- handwriting
- sports
- ball games
- skipping
- riding a bike
- clapping in rhythm
- skipping
- dancing.

Spotting the problems

Sometimes problems with gross and fine motor skills can be spotted at an early age. Other times they only become obvious when the child gets to school. They can result in clumsiness and also make it hard for him to master some important childhood skills. Without the right help, difficulties like these have the potential to impact many areas of his life, particularly at school, and also to damage his self-esteem.

On a more positive note, it is worth keeping in mind that over time motor difficulties become less of a problem. Most children's skills improve as they grow older, at least gradually. And a lot of the skills that are so important in childhood become less important as he gets older. As an adult he will no longer have to contend with compulsory ball games, for example. (See also section on Handwriting, Tips 125–36.)

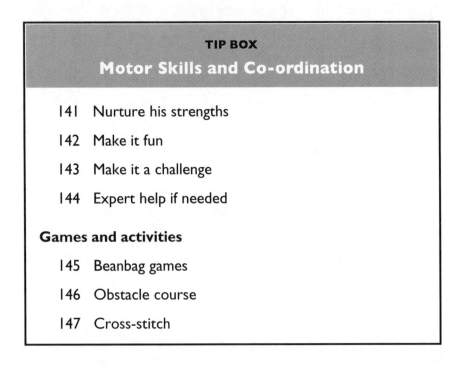

TIP BOX
Motor Skills and Co-ordination

141   Nurture his strengths

142   Make it fun

143   Make it a challenge

144   Expert help if needed

Games and activities

145   Beanbag games

146   Obstacle course

147   Cross-stitch

TIP # 141 Nurture his strengths

Find out what he's good at and nurture his strengths. Start by finding at least one thing to practise that he already does well and build on that. For example, if he is good at catching the ball after you bounce it to him, make a game with that. Build his confidence by focusing on what he does well and enjoys.

TIP # 142 Make it fun

Probably the best way in which we can help is through practice and encouragement. Look for opportunities to allow the child to practise skills such as ball games in a safe place where he is not going to feel embarrassed. Play in the house or garden rather than the park, for example. And don't make practice sessions seem like practice sessions – they should just seem like playing games and having some fun.

TIP # 143 Make it a challenge

Get him motivated to practise by setting a challenge. For example, How many times in a row can you catch the ball when I throw to you? How many times in a row can I catch the ball when you throw to me?

TIP # 144 Expert help if needed

An expert such as an occupational therapist may be able to help by sug-gesting exercises and activities that will help your child with his par-ticular difficulties.

Games and activities

TIP # 145 Beanbag games

A beanbag is fun to play with and a great confidence builder because it is a lot easier to catch than a ball. Games with beanbags can be useful for helping co-ordination.

Start with a very simple throwing and catching game: for example, where the players stand in a circle and one person calls the name of another person and throws the beanbag for him to catch. Start with very easy throws. When he is very confident and has had plenty of practice with the basics, then move on to some 'tricks'. There are endless possibilities of tricks you can do with beanbags. Let the child help 'invent' some tricks and, if he wants, he could even give them some cool names. Here are some ideas to start him off:

- Challenge each other to throw the beanbag upwards and catch it a certain number of times in a row. (Tip – it's a lot easier if you don't throw too high!)
- Throw the beanbag up and jump before catching it.
- Throw the beanbag up and clap before catching it.
- Throw the beanbag up, raise one leg and clap your hand under the raised leg before catching it.

TIP # 146 Obstacle course

As long as you don't mind the disruption inside the house, you can even make an obstacle course indoors, using stools, cushions, etc. And set a course that includes some fun physical challenges. For example:

- walk across the room slowly balancing a beanbag on your head
- up to the top of the stairs and down balancing a beanbag on your head
- three star jumps
- make you way across the hall climbing over each stool as you go
- five situps, etc.

TIP # 147 Cross-stitch

Some children, boys and girls, find cross-stitch fascinating. There is a precision and certainty about it that can be very therapeutic. It is very good for concentration and fine motor skills and can be satisfying and rewarding – especially if you display or frame the results. There are some very appealing, easy patterns available, which are based on popular children's themes.

Perfectionism

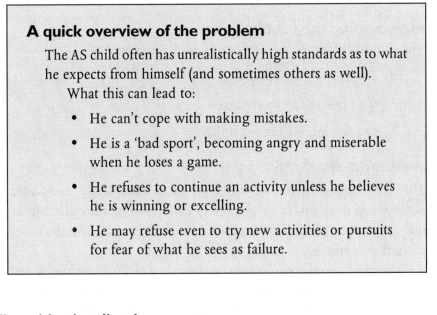

A quick overview of the problem

The AS child often has unrealistically high standards as to what he expects from himself (and sometimes others as well).

What this can lead to:

- He can't cope with making mistakes.
- He is a 'bad sport', becoming angry and miserable when he loses a game.
- He refuses to continue an activity unless he believes he is winning or excelling.
- He may refuse even to try new activities or pursuits for fear of what he sees as failure.

The wider implications

One problem for a child who goes through life with a perfectionist attitude is that he can make life very hard for himself. If he is to have any hope of reaching his own high standards, he will need to drive himself very hard.

On the plus side, having high standards may mean that he produces some high quality work and this may well enhance his career prospects in the future. But the danger of a perfectionist attitude is that he may never attain his own high standards and he may end up facing a lifetime of disappointment.

Another problem is that he can make himself very unpopular. People generally find it hard to cope with a bad sport or a sore loser – he just seems immature and spoilt. Of course we all feel disappointed when we lose, at least to some extent. It's a perfectly normal way to feel. But we usually start to learn to cope with this at quite a young age. We learn that losing is part of life – nobody is perfect – and we can't always win. When we realise this, it helps us to take it in our stride better when we lose or fail. But the same situation can make the AS child extremely upset and provoke an angry reaction.

Understanding the problem

The root of the problem seems to lie in three areas:

- unrealistic expectations
- the craving for acceptance
- the craving for predictability.

UNREALISTIC EXPECTATIONS

The expectations of the AS child are often completely unrealistic. Somewhere deep inside he genuinely expects to 'get it right' all the time. And when inevitably his prediction is not correct, he starts to see himself as a failure.

This negative self-perception can lead to a lack of confidence and motivation. If it becomes very extreme it can even be paralysing, in the sense that he may decide to give up. He may end up refusing even to get involved in any activity where he does not feel absolutely certain of a favourable and predictable outcome.

THE CRAVING FOR ACCEPTANCE

Nobody likes to feel inferior or inadequate, so when the AS child adopts a perfectionist attitude it can be very offputting to other people. It can give the impression that he is deliberately trying to seem superior. It may of course be true that the child is craving a feeling of superiority. But if so, it is important to realise that this is only a substitute for the feelings of acceptance and security he really needs, even though he is not aware of it.

THE CRAVING FOR PREDICTABILITY

Sometimes in order to feel accepted and secure the AS child needs predictability. Being at the extreme end of something is predictable and this often means he wants to be best or first. But apparently even being last can be a distinguished position! My son used to be obsessed with being last out of the classroom every day – not first but LAST! Unless he could be the very last person to exit the room, he would cause a terrible fuss. This caused me many moments of embarrassment, as you can imagine. It was only recently that I came to understand why being last was so important to him. It was one of the few things he felt he could predict and control in the otherwise unpredictable and confusing world of school.

Apathy, perfectionism and fear of failure

Sometimes the AS child seems to vacillate between the two extremes of apathy and perfectionism. It can be quite a puzzle when one day or in one activity, the child is completely apathetic and on another day or in another activity the same child is exceptionally earnest and enthusiastic. Yet in some respects it's not that hard to understand, because there is one way in which the AS child is exactly the same as every other child in the world – he fears failure and hates to be humiliated. But for the AS child, the situation is more difficult. He continually suffers the frustration and humiliation of 'getting it wrong' socially. Additionally, he actually sets himself up for failure and disappointment by the unrealistic standards he sets.

However, although he fears failure, he will probably never admit it. Instead he is likely to avoid the risk of failure completely by withdrawing his co-operation in any area where he is not confident. He will probably say he is not interested, he 'doesn't care', or will simply dig his heels in and refuse to participate.

So in a way apathy can be seen as just the other side of the coin from perfectionism, the philosophy being that: if you can't cope with achieving less than perfection then sometimes it's easier not even to bother trying.

Tackling the problems

We need to encourage the child to set new, more realistic goals for himself. The new standard he needs to learn is that he should aim to do

his *personal best* and then let it go. To teach him this, we need to challenge his way of thinking and gradually teach him a more realistic def-
inition of success.

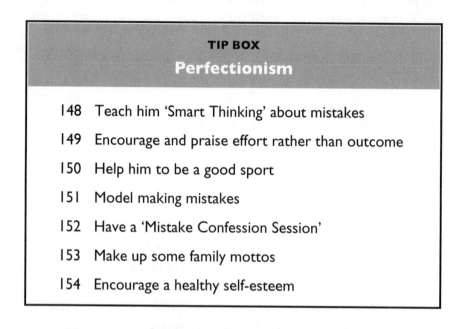

TIP BOX

Perfectionism

148   Teach him 'Smart Thinking' about mistakes

149   Encourage and praise effort rather than outcome

150   Help him to be a good sport

151   Model making mistakes

152   Have a 'Mistake Confession Session'

153   Make up some family mottos

154   Encourage a healthy self-esteem

TIP # 148 Teach him 'Smart Thinking' about mistakes

'Smart Thinking' consists of some perfectly logical ideas, but they may
not occur to the AS child unless you specifically teach them to him. He
will probably not be receptive to taking them on board while he is
actually upset at some 'mistake'. So be on the look out for opportunities when he is relaxed and receptive and gradually introduce him to
some 'Smart Thinking' on the subject of mistakes. For example:

- Everyone has different strengths and weaknesses and that's
  OK.

- Everyone makes mistakes sometimes. There has never been
  a single person in the history of the world who 'got it
  right' every time!

- It's a mature thing to admit your weaknesses and failings.

- Every mistake is a chance to learn how to do something different or better next time.

- Inventors are a good example of patient, smart people who know how to learn from their mistakes. For example, Thomas Edison spent years 'getting it wrong' before he invented the electric light bulb. He tried out literally hundreds of materials trying to find what he was looking for. Once someone asked him if he was not disheartened by having so many failures. He replied that all his efforts were not failures, because each one had taught him something. He now knew hundreds of materials that were definitely not suitable! Eventually he tried tungsten filament and found what he had been looking for. And so the electric lightbulb was invented due to his 'Smart Thinking' attitude to his 'mistakes'.

- Reinforce what you are teaching by letting him read *Mistakes that Worked* (Jones 1994).

TIP # 149 Encourage and praise effort rather than outcome

Teach him that everyone has different abilities and skills. Some people find one thing easy, some another. The most praiseworthy thing is not always the outcome but the effort that a person puts in.

Look out for examples of this and ways to reinforce it in everyday life. For example, if he produces a line of very wobbly handwriting, he may not believe you if you tell him it is beautiful and neat. Try saying something like: 'I like your work. I can see you have applied yourself and put a lot of effort in, and I'm proud of you for that. Remember – effort is what counts. WELL DONE!'

Similarly if there is something that he finds very easy and someone else finds difficult, encourage him to appreciate effort in others. For instance, if his sister is having problems on the computer, tell him that this is something she finds difficult, just like he finds handwriting difficult. Effort is what counts in other people too.

TIP # 150 Help him to be a good sport

He may need to be specifically and patiently taught in words the basic principles that other children gradually learn intuitively, such as:

- Everyone likes to be a winner.

- No one likes to be a loser.

- Not everyone can win and no one can win all the time.

- Losers usually feel disappointed.

- A bad sport makes a fuss when he loses (by stomping off, having a tantrum, or whatever).

- A bad sport 'crows' when he wins (by calling the loser stupid, or whatever).

- A good sport, when he loses, congratulates the winner and says, for instance, 'Well done, Johnnie' and shakes the winner's hand, even though he is disappointed.

- A good sport, when he wins, commiserates with the loser by saying, for instance, 'Well played' or 'It was a close match' or 'Better luck next time.'

At the right moment, such as when he is playing a game, remind him (as well as the other children involved as appropriate) of what you have told them and that you are watching to see if they remember to behave like 'good sports', no matter who wins. They may well forget in the heat of the moment, but praise and congratulate them when they do remember.

TIP # 151 Model making mistakes

Let him see you admitting mistakes and learning from them. They don't need to be important or major mistakes. Even if you forget to post a letter, or if you burn the toast, draw attention to it and say, for instance, 'Oh well, mistakes are cool.'

TIP # 152 Have a 'Mistake Confession Session'

The child needs to learn to think and talk about mistakes in a healthy way and to accept them as part of life. It can be fun to get the whole family involved in this as well, because often the AS child is not the only person in the family who has an immature attitude to mistakes.

In a 'Mistake Confession Session' each person describes some of the mistakes they have made or seen other people making in the past. They also admit how they felt at the time they made the mistake and what they learned from it. Think up, for example:

- embarrassing mistakes
- painful mistakes
- silly mistakes
- serious mistakes
- funny mistakes.

TIP # 153 Make up some family mottos

Have some fun thinking up a family motto. Display it on the kitchen wall or fridge as a reminder. Some suggestions are:

- 'Mistakes are cool.'
- 'The man who never made a mistake never made anything.'

When you see him starting to become upset with himself for making a mistake, remind him of the family motto.

TIP # 154 Encourage a healthy self-esteem

Find ways to encourage the child to have healthy self-esteem so that he feels it's OK to be himself and he doesn't need to be perfect (see Tips 19–23).

Rigidity

A quick overview of the problem

People with Asperger Syndrome find it very hard to be flexible. They can develop a very rigid attitude to many aspects of life. This rigidity is at the root of many typical Asperger traits and accounts for the fact that the typical Asperger child tends to be:

- resistant to change
- stubborn and dogmatic
- obsessive
- pedantic.

What this can lead to:

- He needs to feel he is 'in control', even over the adults in his life, sometimes.
- He needs to feel that life is predictable.
- He sees things as black or white.
- He gets hung up on petty rules.
- He has to be 'right' all the time.
- He likes to establish rituals.
- He finds it difficult to cope with change.
- He becomes absorbed or obsessed with 'special interests'.
- He is pedantic.
- He wastes time arguing minor or silly points.

Resistance to change

The AS child is very resistant to change. Even very minor changes that would not cause a problem for most other children can be difficult for him. Some examples are: changes to his normal routine or schedule; altering the environment he is used to by shifting the furniture in his bedroom; or changes to the people he is used to in his life such as who babysits or collects him from school.

Stubborn and dogmatic

Sometimes with an AS child you can find yourself drawn into an argument without knowing how on earth you got there. When he is in a stubborn mood, he can adopt a very rigid stance. It doesn't matter if the issue involved seems silly, trivial or obscure. If you try to reason with him, it just makes him dig his heels in all the further.

On a side note, it can be funny sometimes when quite a while later you discover him arguing the completely opposite point of view on the same issue equally dogmatically. However this is unlikely to mean that he has been persuaded to change his mind. The chances are that he has just *forgotten* his original position!

It can be very frustrating to deal with a stubborn dogmatic attitude and it is important to recognise and accept it as part of his AS. He is not being deliberately annoying. He genuinely finds it hard to be flexible. When he adopts a particular stance, it is very difficult for him to shift from it. Even if he is clearly mistaken or being completely unreasonable, he finds it very hard to consider any possibility or point of view other than his own. In his mind he is absolutely certain he is right and, if he is in a particularly stubborn mood, no amount of logical reasoning will persuade him even to consider the possibility that he might be wrong.

Obsessions

It's quite normal for children and teenagers to go through 'crazes' when they develop keen interests – perhaps in a favourite TV personality, sport, popstar or fashion. One difference with the AS child is that his area of special interest may be very unusual. Additionally, his interest can become much more absorbing and extensive than normal.

On the plus side, the child may become very knowledgeable about his special interest. If it happens to be an area that his peers are interested in too that can improve his status with them.

However, the downside is that his special interest can develop into an obsession and start to take over his life. He can end up taking it far too seriously and fail to balance it with other interests and pursuits. He may want to talk and think about virtually nothing else and he won't realise that other people don't feel the same way.

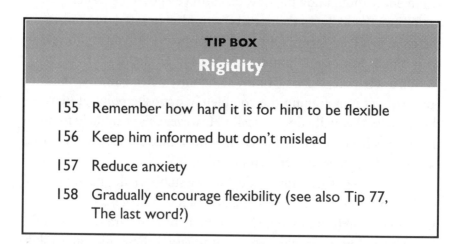

TIP BOX
Rigidity

155   Remember how hard it is for him to be flexible

156   Keep him informed but don't mislead

157   Reduce anxiety

158   Gradually encourage flexibility (see also Tip 77, The last word?)

TIP # 155 Remember how hard it is for him to be flexible

It is hard to keep your patience when your child creates a fuss over something very minor, for example, because he has been asked to get out the 'wrong' door of the car. At such times it can be helpful to remember that rigidity is a very normal part of Asperger Syndrome. It is not just normal 'naughtiness' or bad behaviour. People with Asperger Syndrome find it genuinely difficult to be flexible (see also Tip 15, Understand his rigidity).

TIP # 156 Keep him informed but don't mislead

Keep in mind that from an Asperger point of view the worst thing is the unpredictable. Tell him what the plans and expectations are. Keep a look ahead for any changes that you think he might find difficult and keep him informed of them. He may not like the change, but he will find it a bit easier if he is prepared.

Since knowing what to expect is so important to him, be careful not to make false promises and try, as far as possible, to say exactly what you mean. Don't forget he will probably take what you say very literally, so you may need to use words that don't predict too exactly, like 'probably' and 'usually' and 'about'. This will gradually help him to understand that although you will try to keep him informed, life is not completely predictable.

Tell him for example:

- 'Dad will *probably* collect you from school.'

- 'The bus *usually* comes at 8 am.'

- 'I will be home in *about* half an hour.'

TIP # 157 Reduce anxiety

When he has got into a rigid mindset, remember that getting angry and trying to force him to be flexible are counter-productive. He will be at his most flexible when he is most secure. Any effort that you put in to reduce his anxiety level will be well invested and will ultimately help him learn to be a little more flexible (see Tips 24–34, Reducing Anxiety).

TIP # 158 Gradually encourage flexibility

It is natural that we want to make life comfortable for our AS child by making life more predictable for him. But it is better in the long run if he can become a little more flexible. Sometimes it's a good idea to try to stretch him a bit, by deliberately making a slight change to his pattern. For example, if you usually collect him from school yourself, try one day having someone else collect him instead.

Timing is crucial here because if you push him too far at the wrong time, it may backfire and make him even more rigid. But if you pick a time when he seems relaxed and open to the idea, give him plenty of notice and present it to him in a positive fun way, he may even enjoy the change.

School Issues

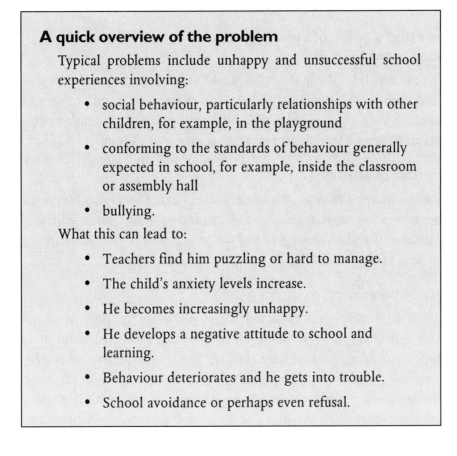

A quick overview of the problem

Typical problems include unhappy and unsuccessful school experiences involving:

- social behaviour, particularly relationships with other children, for example, in the playground
- conforming to the standards of behaviour generally expected in school, for example, inside the classroom or assembly hall
- bullying.

What this can lead to:

- Teachers find him puzzling or hard to manage.
- The child's anxiety levels increase.
- He becomes increasingly unhappy.
- He develops a negative attitude to school and learning.
- Behaviour deteriorates and he gets into trouble.
- School avoidance or perhaps even refusal.

The happiest days of your life?

For a lot of AS children schooldays are definitely not the 'happiest days of your life' that they are supposed to be. If your child is happy and settled at school then that's great, but unfortunately he is probably in the minority. For the sad reality is that all too often children with Asperger Syndrome have a difficult and miserable time at school.

From the teacher's point of view, AS children present quite a challenge. They don't readily conform to school routines and discipline. Their behaviour can be puzzling and exasperating. From the parents' point of view, it can be heartbreaking to watch their children struggle to cope. They are often at their wit's end with worry and frustration. But what's going on from the child's point of view?

The child's point of view

CONFUSION AND CHAOS

To the AS child, the hurly-burly world of school can seem confusing and chaotic. A lot of his difficulty comes from his basic problem of dealing with the unpredictable. Often he genuinely doesn't under-stand either what to expect or what is expected of him.

SENSORY DIFFICULTIES

As he struggles to cope, his anxiety level rises. This makes him more sensitive than usual to sensory stimulus such as noise. Then, when his sensory difficulties are aggravated, he becomes more anxious. And so a vicious cycle can develop.

SOCIAL DIFFICULTIES

Most children love the times when they can enjoy free play. At school this will usually be at lunch or break time. But for the AS child these are often the most difficult times of all. They don't quite know how to get along with their peers in unstructured, unsupervised playtime. They have very little understanding of many of the games and social concepts that most children pick up easily, especially where they involve teams, groups or 'gangs'. Difficulties like these leave him wide open to bullying and teasing.

OTHER FACTORS

Additionally, in the classroom he may have difficulties with:

- handwriting (see Tips 125–36)
- attention, concentration and organisation (see Tips 88–95)
- completion of homework (see Tips 137–40).

Bullying: AS child as victim, perceived victim or perpetrator

Although the problem of bullying is sadly not confined to school, this is usually the place where the AS child is at his most vulnerable. Bullying is a distressing problem for any child, but for the child with Asperger Syndrome the situation is a lot more difficult and complex.

AS CHILD AS VICTIM OR PERCEIVED VICTIM OF BULLYING

Tony Attwood (1998) describes school as a 'social minefield' for AS children. They tend to bring out either the maternal or the predatory instinct in other children. Some children feel the urge to mother and look after them but others unfortunately regard them as 'prey' and treat them in a mean and nasty way.

The AS child is poorly equipped to recognise the 'predators' let alone defend himself against them. He cannot easily 'mind read' the intentions of other people so it is hard for him to know who is a real friend and who is not. This leaves him open to two main problems:

1. His vulnerability is taken advantage of and he is subject to mean and unfair treatment. In this situation he actually *becomes* a victim of bullying.

2. He misinterprets the intentions of people who mean him no harm and overreacts, for example, to joking or teasing comments that are meant innocently or in fun. When this happens he *misperceives himself* as a victim of bullying or mistreatment.

It is important to remember that these two problems are *both equally real and upsetting* in the mind of the child with Asperger Syndrome.

AS CHILD AS PERPETRATOR OF BULLYING

The child with Asperger Syndrome is unlikely ever to engage in a subtle campaign of bullying. But on the other hand sometimes he can throw his weight about just like any other child. Typically this will tend to happen in a spontaneous rather than a premeditated way, for example, when he is acting out his own frustrations and anger.

In general the AS child is more likely than the average child to be a victim rather than a perpetrator of bullying. And whenever he does engage in bullying, he is more likely to be caught and get into trouble. In fact he is easy prey to be deliberately provoked or set up for this kind of thing to happen.

THE DAMAGE THAT BULLYING CAN DO

No matter what the circumstances, bullying can be a serious problem for the AS child and can make his life very miserable. This can manifest in various ways including the following:

- Self-esteem and confidence suffer.
- He becomes depressed and withdrawn.
- He becomes hostile and angry.
- Levels of anxiety and tension increase.
- Motivation declines.

Attitude to school

Apparently in the mind of the average child, school is as much as 85 per cent to do with socialising with their friends. Other things such as lessons are only 15 per cent of what is important in his mind. The danger is that in the mind of the AS child, school might become 85 per cent about negative feelings and experiences: of failure, rejection, humiliation, being misunderstood, unfairly treated or bullied. Without the right support it is very easy for his motivation to suffer. He can develop a negative attitude to school and learning and drift into a position where he decides it's not even worth bothering to try.

On a more positive note

It is worth keeping in mind that even though schooldays are very important, they don't last for ever. Life after school may be a lot easier for a person with Asperger Syndrome. The degree of conformity expected of him during the school years does eventually come to an end. And when he is older he should be freer to arrange his life in a way that is easier for him. He will able to follow his own interests, to avoid noisy groups, to choose the social setting which suits him best and to structure his working life in a way that fits in with his personality.

Tackling the problems

Once we have left our child inside the school gates we have, in effect, entrusted his care and responsibility to the school authorities, and they will of course have their own rules and procedures. As parents, our influence on how the child experiences school is therefore limited, but there are still a lot of ways in which we can help him.

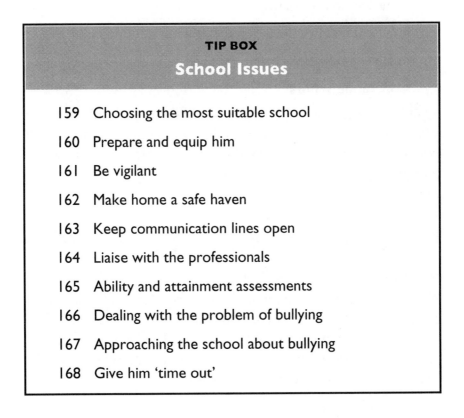

TIP BOX

School Issues

159   Choosing the most suitable school

160   Prepare and equip him

161   Be vigilant

162   Make home a safe haven

163   Keep communication lines open

164   Liaise with the professionals

165   Ability and attainment assessments

166   Dealing with the problem of bullying

167   Approaching the school about bullying

168   Give him 'time out'

TIP # 159 Choosing the most suitable school

The first and most important decision that needs to be made is which school will suit your child best. When you are investigating and visiting schools, it can be hard to know what factors you should be looking out for. The right school to suit an AS child can be hard to find. Ideally it will:

- have a quiet, orderly atmosphere
- be prepared to be open and flexible
- be sympathetic to the needs of the child
- have a sound knowledge of Asperger Syndrome, or at least be prepared to learn
- have a good positive experience with other AS children
- have good ratios of staff to pupils
- be caring yet firm.

If you can get speaking to the parents of another AS child from the same school this can be very helpful. They can tell you what their experience has been. Some schools may not mind setting up such a contact for you if you request it. A personal recommendation can be very reassuring.

TIP # 160 Prepare and equip him

'NORMAL' PREPARATION FOR SCHOOL

When any child is starting school it is a great help to him if he knows in advance what to expect from a normal schoolday. For the AS child this is even more important. Take steps to prepare him in a realistic, positive and fun way. Talk to him about school and carry out activities and games involving the theme of school:

- Read books.
- Watch videos.

- Draw pictures.
- Play 'school' (role play).
- Take him to see the school and teacher.

EQUIPPING HIM SOCIALLY FOR SCHOOL

The AS child has many extra difficulties to cope with, especially in the area of social skills, so it is only fair that he gets extra preparation to help him deal with these. Anything you can do to *help him with his social skills and social awareness* will be of great benefit to him in school (see Tips 35–50, Bridging the Social and Emotional Gap).

It is easy to assume he understands more than he does. Help him to understand some of the subtle concepts that may help him to cope in the social minefield of school:

- Hurting is Not Always Intentional (Appendix 11).
- Teasing and Banter (Appendix 12).

TIP # 161 Be vigilant

Keep an eye on how happy or unhappy he seems to be at school. If he wants to tell you about a problem, try to listen patiently. However, he may not always find it easy to talk so you may need to look for clues:

- How does he seem going into school? Is he reluctant and nervous or keen and relaxed?
- How does he seem to be interacting with other children? Keep in touch with the teacher on this point.
- How does he seem at weekends and holidays? Is he much more relaxed at these times?
- Are there signs that might indicate physical bullying such as bruising, cuts, torn clothes or 'lost' dinner money? (See also Tip 167 below.)

If he is unhappy at school this may manifest in:

- insomnia
- anxiety
- aggression
- moodiness and bad temper
- being quiet and withdrawn
- reluctance to attend.

TIP # 162 Make home a safe haven

Because school can be very difficult for the AS child, he really needs home to be somewhere he feels safe. It is vital that he has at least one place where he can relax and where he feels he has got someone on his side. One good way of helping him feel supported is by simply giving him a listening ear (see Tip 107, Empathic listening).

He may often feel he is unfairly treated at school and so it is even more important that at home you are not only fair but also seen to be so. You may need to supervise quite closely to try and prevent tensions being played out between children after they come home from school.

TIP # 163 Keep communication lines open

Do what you can to keep communication lines open between yourself and the school. Keep in touch with the teacher and ask him or her to let you know if there are any problems. If there are difficulties at home send in a note. It is easier for the school if they know what is going on at home and vice versa.

When there is a problem at school it can be difficult to get to the bottom of it and find out what is really going on. Usually the child and the school will both agree that things are not going well, but each will have a different point of view as to *what* is wrong. This can be very hard to navigate through. Try to hear both sides of the story as fairly as you can.

If you feel the child is out of line, remember the goal is to 'love the child, but challenge the behaviour'. Try to let him know that although you do not accept his behaviour, you still love and accept him and want to help him behave differently next time.

If you feel the school has been wrong or unfair it can be difficult to handle. Try talking to them openly and honestly. Tell them how you feel: that you are very concerned; that you realise your child can be difficult to manage; that you are not trying to judge what happened; and that you would love to hear what is going on from the school's point of view. Remember that a confrontational attitude usually does more harm than good.

Often the school will be able to explain things and reassure you that they are doing their best, just as you are doing your best. If they are open to suggestions they may be very glad of any ideas you have as to how things might be handled differently next time. (See also Tip 167, Approaching the school about bullying.)

TIP # 164 Liaise with the professionals

Whether or not your child has a diagnosis when he starts school, before too long he will probably come to the attention of the school and education authorities as a child who needs some special attention. Eventually he may need some professional assessment and help. Often the AS child has quite a number of different difficulties, which means that you may end up having to liaise with a variety of professionals.

Managing all this as well as managing your AS child at home can seem very daunting, but think of yourself as part of a team of experts. *You are an expert on your own child* and know him in a way that no one else does. The child will be best served if you can develop and foster good relationships with the staff and other professionals. Remember you are all on the same side and that parents are an essential part of the team.

TIP # 165 Ability and attainment assessments

The school may want to have the child undergo various tests as part of their assessment procedure. It can be interesting to see what these reveal because, even though we know our own child very well, tests can allow us to see them from a different angle. Ideally assessment should reveal specific strengths as well as weaknesses and give a fuller picture, which will allow appropriate help to be put in place.

IQ tests on children with Asperger Syndrome can have surprising results. There can be a 'jagged' score, whereby they score unusually high in some areas and low on others. A low score may not necessarily be a reliable indication of ability, because if you happen to get an AS child on a 'bad day' he may underperform or refuse to co-operate. So the result may not always reveal his true potential.

Getting a second or private opinion is worth considering if you feel it would give a more accurate picture. But on the other hand you don't want to put the child through too many stressful ordeals.

A SPLIT ASSESSMENT?

Lengthy assessments can be tough on a child. It is sometimes possible for a test to be split over two days. If you think a long assessment is likely to put him under too much strain, it is at least worth asking about this possibility.

TIP # 166 Dealing with the problem of bullying

If you suspect that your child is either being bullied or in danger of being bullied, here are some steps you could take:

1. Make sure he knows and understands what bullying is and how he should handle it. See:

    ○ What is Bullying? (Appendix 13)
    ○ Bullying Dos and Don'ts (Appendix 14)

2. Keep him out of danger and away from people you are suspicious about if you can. Identify bullying 'hotspots'

such as the school bus and find a way to avoid these p.
at least while the matter is being investigated or resolved.

3. If he complains that he has been mistreated or bullied,
    calmly listen to him and do not make light of his concerns in
    any way. Tell him he has done the right thing to talk to you
    and help him know that you are on his side and that you
    believe him. It is very important for him to know you care
    and that bullying will be taken seriously by the adults in his
    life.

4. Try to get as truthful an account as possible. You may need
    to speak to other people as well if the situation warrants it.
    If the child admits any details that are not in his favour,
    such as that he provoked the incident in some way,
    remember to praise him for his honesty.

5. Don't jump to conclusions. Children with Asperger
    Syndrome tend to misperceive interactions and so the
    situation may be less straightforward than it appears. Try to
    establish calmly whether this is a case of oversensitivity or
    genuine bullying. If it seems that the problem is one of
    oversensitivity rather than actual bullying, take this as a clue
    that the child's self-esteem may be at a low ebb. If this is
    the case he needs to feel that you are on his side more than
    ever at this point, even if his bullying concerns are not
    realistic.

6. If you suspect that he is being bullied but he is not
    forthcoming about it, you may want to try and investigate.
    In order to get a feel for what is going on you might be
    able to have an informal word with the teacher. Or you
    could ask your child some of the following questions:

    ○ How did school go today?
    ○ What were the best/worst parts of the day?
    ○ Who did you play with?
    ○ What games did you play?

- Did you enjoy them?
- Who did you play with?
- Who do you like best at school?
- Who do you like least?
- Why?
- Are you looking forward to going to school tomorrow?

7. Keep a diary of what happens and what the child says in case the situation requires further action.

8. If appropriate take the child to the doctor so that he can assess the situation and make an official record of the child's distress.

9. Notify the school or the person or body in authority as appropriate.

TIP # 167 Approaching the school about bullying

Contact the school (or other people in authority) if you are sufficiently concerned about a bullying issue. If you think the matter is urgent tell them so and try to get an appointment as soon as possible. When you subsequently attend any meetings in the school the following points are helpful:

- Make a note of the items you want to discuss.
- Consider taking along your partner or a friend as a support or to help you remember what is said.
- Be firm but polite. Getting into an argument is unlikely to help.
- Do not blame, exaggerate or jump to conclusions.
- Ask them what they have noticed and what action they would suggest.
- Make your own suggestions.

- If there is a problem that just involves one other child, suggest that contact between the two children might be monitored for a while.

- Make sure you understand what action the school intends to take.

- Arrange to contact them at a later stage so that you can follow up the situation.

TIP # 168 Give him 'time out'

SCHEDULED BREAKS

If a child seems to be getting over-anxious for whatever reason, consider giving him what Tony Attwood (1998) calls a 'mental health break'; in other words a short time away from school when he does his work at home. Try to negotiate this with the school and keep them informed.

PERMANENT 'TIME OUT' – HOME SCHOOLING

Home schooling a child is a huge undertaking and definitely not to be undertaken lightly. Whether it is a good idea depends very much on the individual case (see Tips 137–40, Homework Supervision, for ideas for working with a child at home). Unless you have a lot of support it can be a very lonely and isolating experience. If you are thinking about it the Home Education Advisory Service is an excellent source of advice and information. (PO Box 98, Welwyn Garden City, Hertfordshire AL8 6AN.)

The most obvious and important advantage of home schooling is the reduction of anxiety in extreme cases. But realistically speaking there are many major factors that you need to consider:

- The strain on yourself and your family.

- The risk of becoming insular and obsessed with your child.

- It becomes more difficult to have a life of your own.

- It may be hard to find opportunities for him to practise social skills.

- He may be extremely difficult to motivate, interest and teach.

- It is a lot for one person to take on, especially if they are untrained, inexperienced and very tired.

- It is hard to combine the roles of parent and teacher.

- It may be very difficult to drag him away from a lot of temptations at home such as TV and computer games.

Sensory Issues

A quick overview of the problem

A child with Asperger Syndrome may have an unusual sensitivity to certain sensory experiences such as sound and touch. For example, he may find it hard to tolerate:

- certain sounds
- crowds
- textures in, for example, certain clothing and labels
- or he may have an abnormal experience of pain or temperature.

What this can lead to:

- Anxiety levels increase.
- Behaviour deteriorates – especially if the child's difficulties are not recognised and so no allowances are made.

The child's point of view

Heightened or distorted sensory experiences are very common in people with Asperger Syndrome. Some of their autobiographies are useful in helping us understand a bit more about what this is like for them. Yet even though sensory difficulties are quite common, they can easily not be picked up.

One reason is that the child will not always tell you that he is experiencing anything unusual because of course from his perspective it's not anything unusual. He has no way of knowing that what he is experiencing is any different from anyone else.

Given that these difficulties are not always obvious, it may be worth keeping a discreet look out for them. They could be a cause or contributory factor in anxiety and poor behaviour that is otherwise unexplained.

Some common sensitivities

SOUNDS

Some of the sounds he may be sensitive to include:

- sudden, unexplained or very loud noises
- background type sounds such as the hustle and bustle of a crowd
- the sound of applause
- other specific sounds such as a baby crying or a vacuum cleaner.

TOUCH

This sensitivity may show up as hating to cuddle or even to brush against other people, for example, when lining up with other children in school. Or he may be intolerant of minor annoyances like a clothing label against his skin.

At the other extreme or at different times, he may crave the sensation of deep pressure or being 'squashed'. In order to satisfy this craving he may initiate rough or inappropriate physical contact. As regards horseplay and being tickled, it is likely that he will either absolutely love or hate them.

TEMPERATURE

He may not have much sensitivity to temperature. This can mean it is hard to persuade him to wear warm clothes in cold weather or to take off heavy clothes when it is warm.

PAIN

He may have either a very high or a very low threshold of pain. If his threshold is high it will be less obvious, meaning he could be sick or in pain without knowing it.

EATING DIFFICULTIES

See Tips 111–24.

OTHER

He may either crave or detest the spinning sensation that you get from twirling, playground rides or even rollercoasters.

Understanding the problem

Perhaps the only way in which 'normal' people can understand sensory difficulties is by realising that not everybody experiences sensory stimuli in exactly the same way. Of course there are many things that most of us would agree on. Most people enjoy the taste of chocolate, for example. But other sensations are very individual.

Think of the sound of someone scraping his fingernails down a blackboard. A lot of people really hate that sound and find it almost painful. I've seen people cover their ears if they hear it even for a moment. If it were prolonged maybe they would feel like running out of the room to avoid it. Yet for others like myself it's just an ordinary sound. I can see no logical reason why it should bother anyone.

This is a bit similar to how 'normal' people sometimes feel about people with Asperger Syndrome. We just don't understand why certain things bother them. Maybe we just have to accept that they do.

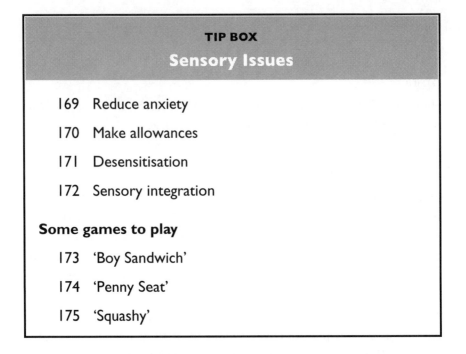

TIP BOX

Sensory Issues

169   Reduce anxiety

170   Make allowances

171   Desensitisation

172   Sensory integration

Some games to play

173   'Boy Sandwich'

174   'Penny Seat'

175   'Squashy'

TIP # 169 Reduce anxiety

There would appear to be some connection between an Asperger child's level of sensory tolerance and his anxiety level. When he is less anxious he seems to experience fewer difficulties and vice versa. So to some extent his sensitivity can be seen as a barometer of his anxiety level at any given time. Take general steps to reduce anxiety, especially during times when the child is especially sensitive (see Tips 24–34).

TIP # 170 Make allowances

Keep a look out for sensory experiences the child may find difficult, and be prepared to allow him to avoid situations where you think he is likely to be very uncomfortable.

TIP # 171 Desensitisation

At times when he is less anxious, look for ways to stretch his tolerance very gently. The aim is gradually to desensitise him to the stimulus that he finds so difficult. For example, if, as my son had, he has difficulties with the noise of the vacuum cleaner, pick a moment when he is feeling happy, calm and confident and let him hear it for a short period of time and at a distance. Praise and congratulate him on coping with it, but don't push him too far on that occasion. *The main thing is that he should feel successful.*

Next time try building on his earlier success by letting it run for longer or in a nearer room, and so on. Eventually he will be able to say proudly, 'The noise of the hoover *used* to bother me when I was younger but not any more.'

TIP # 172 Sensory integration

See a sensory integration specialist to assess and diagnose the nature and extent of the sensory problems. He or she may offer various types of help, or perhaps offer to give your child a massage. You may even want to learn how to do this yourself for your child and the specialist could give you some pointers on how best to do this. He or she may also offer advice and recommend some remedial excercises.

Some games to play

He may benefit from playing games that allow him to experience the sensation of pressure. Here are some examples of the kind of games that can be fun and therapeutic, but of course there are countless possibilities that you can make up yourself:

TIP # 173 'Boy Sandwich'

The child lies on the floor on top of a duvet or quilt, and gets lots of layers of heavy quilts, cushions and covers piled on top of him. (Don't cover his face of course!) He may like it even better if you apply some pressure to the 'sandwich' when it is made.

TIP # 174 'Penny Seat'

Two adults make a 'seat' for the child to sit in by facing each other and linking crossed-over hands. The child gets a 'ride' in the seat, but every time they come to a doorway, the adults pretend that there is not enough room. So the 'penny seat' gets stuck for quite a few moments in the doorway with the child on the seat getting very squashed in the middle. (Giving the child a ride on a 'penny seat' into his bedroom can be a good way to encourage him to go there in the evening!)

TIP # 172 'Squashy'

The child sits on a sofa or easy chair and the adult 'accidentally' goes to sit on top of him, gradually lowering his weight gently down, while of course making sure not to overdo it. (You need to make sure the child's squeals are still squeals of pleasure, not pain!)

Special Events, Social Occasions and Outings

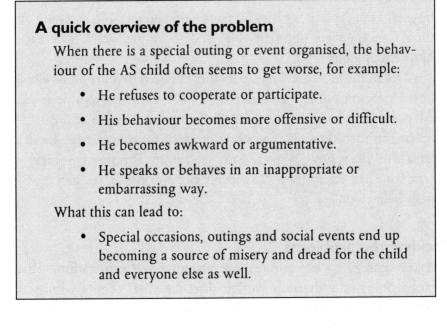

A quick overview of the problem

When there is a special outing or event organised, the behaviour of the AS child often seems to get worse, for example:

- He refuses to cooperate or participate.
- His behaviour becomes more offensive or difficult.
- He becomes awkward or argumentative.
- He speaks or behaves in an inappropriate or embarrassing way.

What this can lead to:

- Special occasions, outings and social events end up becoming a source of misery and dread for the child and everyone else as well.

'Special' events

When there is something 'special' happening – for example: a holiday; perhaps some visitors arriving; a gathering of family and friends; maybe a special outing – these are times when we want and expect our children to have a good time and of course we hope they'll be on their best behaviour too.

But parents of AS children soon find that these are the very times when their AS children are likely to be miserable and on their worst behaviour.

'IS THIS SUPPOSED TO BE FUN?'

'Normal' children usually love a special occasion. Even the very idea of something like a holiday, going out to visit friends or relations, or going to a show or party fills them with happy feelings of excitement and anticipation. And then the special occasion itself is usually a positive, fun experience for them.

But for the AS child, it's very different. Special occasions can be very stressful. This is not really hard to understand when you consider he gets so much of his security from life being predictable. 'Exciting' to the AS child equals 'unpredictable', and the unpredictable can make him very anxious.

A lot of the happy feelings that other children have are replaced by horrible feelings of fear or dread. So it's not surprising that he seems reluctant when he anticipates a 'special' occasion. His fear of the unfamiliar can then dominate the occasion itself for him and he doesn't have 'fun' the way we want and expect him to. This negative experience can then easily lead to a vicious circle of dread, resistance and poor behaviour.

Tackling the problems

A key strategy is clear and realistic planning and expectations. This means doing some detective work to discover what has gone wrong on previous occasions so you can take it into account. It also means preparing the child for the occasion in an honest and realistic way so that he knows what to expect.

TIP BOX

Special Events, Social Occasions and Outings

176 Honest previews

177 Have a 'Back-up Plan'

178 Be early

179 Feedback, praise and encouragement

180 Have a signal or code

Ideas for the car journey

181 Have a rota

182 A map

183 An itinerary

184 Schedule stops

185 Tape

186 Reading

187 'Dummy's Meeting'

188 Do a survey

189 Twenty Questions, etc.

190 Puzzle books

TIP # 176 Honest previews

Let him know that his anxieties and difficulties are accepted and understood and don't make little of the problems he is likely to face. If there is something he is probably going to find hard and you tell him 'It won't be so bad' he is likely to distrust what you say next time.

On the other hand, if you are honest with him, he will feel understood and respected and it will help him trust you the next time. Tell him, for example: 'There are some parts of the evening I would expect you to enjoy, but I think you will find some things difficult. When we arrive, there will probably be a crowd of about 15 people. They will all be chatting to each other and making a lot of noise. I think you are probably going to hate that bit. I hope you can manage it OK. Later on there will be some chocolate cake and coke and I think you will enjoy that.'

TIP # 177 Have a 'Back-up Plan'

Have a 'Back-up Plan' so the child knows he has some options if he is finding things too much. Often simply letting the child know that he has a choice helps him to cope. Agree the 'Back-up Plan' in advance, for example: 'When the guests are here, you must come and say hello to them. I'd like you to do your best to stay for a while, but you can go to your room and watch TV if you are very uncomfortable.'

TIP # 178 Be early

If certain social events cause problems, try going early enough to be the first, so your child has the opportunity to 'get the lie of the land' before many other people turn up. Arriving late, on the other hand, may be very stressful, because the child has to cope with a new environment and a new set of people all at once.

TIP # 179 Feedback, praise and encouragement

It may be a great help to the child if he gets some sort of feedback from you, while he is in company, to let him know he is doing OK.

TIP # 180 Have a signal or code

When you are in company, It can be hard for you to know when he is becoming over-anxious, uncomfortable or needs your attention. It can also be hard for you to correct him when his behaviour is getting out of line without causing embarrassment. Think up a signal that you can use (see Tip 71). It might be a good idea to let your host or guests know about the signal in advance so that if needs be you can more easily excuse yourself.

Ideas for the car journey

Car journeys with any children can be very stressful when they are demanding attention, refusing to sit still and bickering over the slightest thing. And the problems can be more extreme when one of them has Asperger Syndrome. You need to have a range of strategies to fall back on.

TIP # 181 Have a rota

When children are hot and bothered, it's amazing what they can find to squabble about. If you have the problem of constant bickering over minor issues such as who is sitting where in the car, be careful not to give in too often to the AS child. If it seems that you always let him have his way when he kicks up a fuss, this can seem very unfair to other children. They can feel as if they are being penalised for behaving well, which is of course the wrong message and can lead to resentment.

These minor issues can be very important to children. Plan ahead, so that everyone is very clear about what is happening in advance. Put a rota on the noticeboard if need be, so the system can be seen to be fair to all.

TIP # 182 A map

Make the journey a bit more interesting by bringing along a map. If you don't have one, draw a rough map, or you could print one off from the internet. The AS child or children can follow the map and look out for landmarks and signposts.

TIP # 183 An itinerary

Prepare a simple itinerary with rough estimates of times, so the child knows what to expect, for example:

Leave home: approx. 10.30 am

Drive to Bill's house: approx. 30 minutes journey time

Collect Bill: approx. 11.00 am

Drive to McDonald's: arrive approx. 12.00

Have lunch: approx. 12.00 till 12.30

Continue journey to Granny's house, arriving approx.1.30 pm

TIP # 184 Schedule stops

If the journey is to be very long, break it up a bit by scheduling some stops into the itinerary, at specific times or places. Use the stops for something like 'stretching your legs' or having a snack or even a picnic meal or outdoor game.

TIP # 185 Tape

Bring along a music or story tape to listen to or sing along with.

TIP # 186 Reading

Some people are nauseated when they try to read in a moving car. As long as the child does not have that problem, bring along a favourite book for him to read to pass the time.

TIP# 187 'Dummy's Meeting'

To get a period of peace and quiet for yourself when you are driving, try calling a 'Dummy's Meeting' where the first person to speak is 'out'.

TIP # 188 Do a survey

Bring along some notebooks and carry out a 'survey'. Decide in advance what you will survey. Some examples are:

- favourite vehicles
- cars (or vans or trucks, etc.) of a particular colour
- cars of a particular make
- cars with a particular type of registration.

Another idea which can be fun is to score vehicles according to how well kept and clean they are!

TIP # 189 Twenty Questions, etc.

Play games such as 'I Spy' or 'Twenty Questions'.

How do you play 'Twenty Questions'? Basically one person thinks of an object and the others have to guess what it is. At the start they give one piece of information, for example, 'It is an object in the front of the car.' The others are allowed to ask a maximum of 20 questions before guessing what it is. For example, 'Is it on the floor?' 'Does it belong to me?' 'Is it a toy?' Is it large?' They can only receive a yes or no answer to their questions.

TIP # 190 Puzzle books

Bring along some puzzle books, dot-to-dot, crosswords, word puzzles, etc. depending on his interest and what he's likely to be motivated to do.

Speech and Conversation

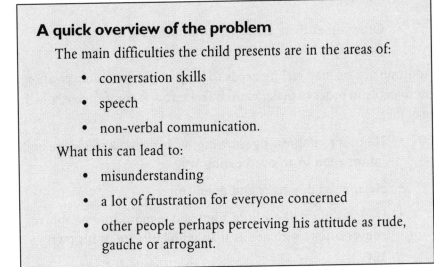

A quick overview of the problem

The main difficulties the child presents are in the areas of:

- conversation skills
- speech
- non-verbal communication.

What this can lead to:

- misunderstanding
- a lot of frustration for everyone concerned
- other people perhaps perceiving his attitude as rude, gauche or arrogant.

Speech

Some AS children have a perfectly normal speaking voice. Others can develop an affected or strange way of speaking. For example, they might use a monotonous tone or perhaps a foreign accent, or speak unusually slowly or unusually fast.

Conversation skills

Sometimes it seems hard to have a normal, relaxed conversation with an AS child and yet it's hard to put your finger on exactly why. It's as if there isn't the easygoing 'to-and-fro' that you would normally expect.

The lack of empathy which AS people are noted for means he may not realise that other people are not interested in the same things as he is, so, for example:

- He is rigid and inflexible, getting stuck on a particular topic, and it is hard to get the subject changed. He doesn't pick up the subtle clues that indicate that other people are getting bored (or perhaps even intimidated).

- Sometimes he talks on and on and it seems as if there is no 'off switch'.

- Other times there are long, uncomfortable delays when he doesn't reply and we are not sure why.

Additionally, he may feel he needs to keep control in a conversation, presumably in order to make himself feel safe and comfortable, which may mean:

- He tries to impress by showing off his wide knowledge and information in an overbearing way.

- He appears dogmatic and dominant.

- He talks more like a little adult and is more comfortable in conversations with adults than with children of his own age.

Tackling the problems

The AS child needs to be taught certain things about communication that most other children know intuitively:

- There are unwritten rules to the art of conversation.

- What people say is not always exactly the same as what they mean.

TIP BOX
Speech and Conversation

191 Communicate clearly

192 Leave him a thinking gap

193 Teach him 'rescue phrases'

194 Have a firm boundary

Some games and activities

195 Beanbag games

196 Rhymes and tongue twisters

197 Reading aloud

198 An answerphone message

199 Use a tape recorder

200 The Clear Speech game

TIP # 191 Communicate clearly

Model for him the kind of speaking voice that you would like to hear him use, that is clear, articulate, pleasant and polite (see also Tip 53).

TIP # 192 Leave him a thinking gap

Most people find periods of silence or 'gaps' in a conversation a bit uncomfortable. When you ask an AS child a question, there may be such a gap. Often 'normal people' respond to this by trying to somehow fill in the gap, for example:

- We repeat the question in a different way.

- We guess the answer and ask him to confirm it.

- We check have we been heard.
- We prompt a reply.

If there is a gap in conversation with an AS child, it may mean he needs time to think because he is not sure of how to reply. Sometimes this happens because in his mind he feels he has to give an accurate answer, even where none is needed. For example, if you meet an AS child during the school holidays, in order to try and be friendly you might say: 'Hi, Michael. When did you finish for the holiday?' You could well be met with a stoney silence. Why? Perhaps because the child is trying to remember exactly when he finished so he can give an accurate answer. He misses the point that this is just 'small talk' and the answer doesn't have to be precise. Most other children could easily give an inexact answer like 'A few days ago' or even 'Some time last week, I think.' At times like these it can be better not to interrupt the gap and instead to give him those extra few moments of uninterrupted thinking time that he needs to formulate a reply.

TIP # 193 Teach him 'rescue phrases'

Explain to him that other people feel uncomfortable with gaps in the conversation. It may not be logical, but it is true. So when he is not sure what to say, it is a good idea for him to have a few 'rescue phrases' to fall back upon, for example:

- 'Let me think for a moment'
- 'I'm not sure'
- 'I'll have to think'
- 'Let me see'
- 'I don't know'
- Or teach him that it's often OK to give an approximate answer like: 'It was about a week ago.'

TIP # 194 Have a firm boundary

When he is 'in your face', talking incessantly about a particular topic such as his special interest, and you are getting bored or fed up with listening, be absolutely direct rather than subtle. Instead of dropping a hint, which will probably be lost on him, calmly say something like, 'I will listen to you just for another five minutes. Then I am going to read the paper' or even 'I must go. I can't listen to you any more just now.'

Some games and activities

TIP # 195 Beanbag games

Beanbags can be fun because they are easy to catch and feel good to play with. They can be used to help make speech games fun. Play a game where there is only one beanbag and whoever is holding it must 'make a funny speech' on a chosen topic. Or perhaps whoever catches the beanbag has to say a tongue twister. A timer can be used to time the 'speeches' or tongue twisters.

Tip # 196 Rhymes and Tongue twisters

To encourage confidence in verbal skills, especially if the child is having difficulties with certain sounds, encourage him to recite favourite rhymes. (The verses of Roald Dahl appeal to a lot of children.)

Or have some fun with tongue twisters! For example

She sells sea shells on the sea shore.'

Search on the Internet for rhymes and tongue twisters which might appeal to your child. There are some funny and interesting ones out there!

Or why not make up some of your own?

TIP # 197 Reading aloud

To help him practise speaking clearly, it can be fun to take turns reading aloud, perhaps from a favourite storybook. This can allow you to identify what problems there are in his speech, if any. It also allows you to model clear speech for him.

TIP # 198 An answerphone message

Let him prepare a message to leave on the telephone answering machine. You may need to help him prepare what to say, write it out for him and let him practise it a few times before recording it. (If there are other children in the family, it is only fair to let each of them have a turn at different times.)

TIP # 199 Use a tape recorder

Have fun taping each other or making up games to help him in specific areas. For example, if he tends to speak too quickly, you could play 'Which sounds better?' Try letting him hear how his voice sounds at different rates and praise him when he improves.

TIP # 200 The Clear Speech game

If the child has a lazy, unclear or idiosyncratic way of speaking, play the Clear Speech game (see Appendix 10).

4

A Word of Personal Reflection

The Gift

What I Have Learned

Planet Asperger

Report from Planet Asperger

The Gift

Having a child with Asperger Syndrome was not something I bargained for. It is by far the hardest job I have ever done and it has changed my life completely. There are times when I get worn out, frustrated and depressed, and I feel just like giving up. But I wouldn't swap my child for the world and I bet you feel the same about your child. In my higher moments I know that if I could go back in time and start all over, I would do it all again. I would choose my son in a heartbeat.

I suppose we all like to make our mark on the world, but we'd rather do it on our own terms. It is easier to put our effort into doing something the world recognises and rewards. And yet what is there more worthwhile and fulfilling than helping another person to become truly happy and free?

The opportunity to care for special children is a wonderful gift and a privilege. Every AS parent has a unique and worthwhile task, the chance to make a difference and the chance to learn so much. Nothing happens by mistake; there are no accidents. Special children come to special people. Or is it that the special task can help us see our specialness?

What I Have Learned

Like very young children, people with Asperger Syndrome don't play the same social games as the rest of us. Many of these games are designed to help us hide bits of ourselves. So it's no wonder that interacting with AS people can make us feel uncomfortable. Honesty is quite a challenge, but it's also a chance to look afresh at our comfortable ways of thinking and relating. And we can learn a lot when we are dragged from our comfort zones!

I have learned a lot of things I never would have otherwise known. I've learned to see life differently. I've learned to think more carefully about what I say and how I act and to keep on trying something new. I've learned to be more patient – which can't be a bad thing. I've met wonderful people who have inspired me and helped me learn what matters in life.

The more I learn about Asperger Syndrome, the more fascinated I become. I've come to the conclusion that AS people have a very extreme version of traits that are, to some extent, in every one of us. This means that understanding Asperger Syndrome can help us understand more about each other and ourselves. I am proud to admit that I have a lot of Asperger traits too. And I like myself a lot better now that I have got to know and have embraced those parts of myself.

Planet Asperger

Sometimes people with AS say they feel literally as if they are on the wrong planet and that they don't fit in on this one. Did you ever find yourself wondering what it would be like in a place where they did fit in?

Imagine if there was another planet where Asperger Syndrome was the norm and where AS people felt they really did belong. What would it be like, do you think? It is interesting to consider that it would probably be kinder, safer and more truthful than this world. If we could send an anthropologist there to visit, what kind of a report would he bring back? Perhaps it would read something like this.

REPORT FROM PLANET ASPERGER

On Planet Asperger humanity has evolved quite differently and some of the scourges of our world which result from human cruelty and deceit are completely unknown. People highly value individuality, space, privacy and freedom from coercion. The phenomenon of group behaviour, such as the tendency to organise into social groups and follow a leader, is virtually absent. This has had very far-reaching implications. War, for example is completely unknown.

The inhabitants tend to have a keen sense of fair play. Their laws are based on clear moral standards, although specific regulations can be unduly complicated. Highly developed computer technology facilitates much of the communication. When people come together socially it is usually for a specific reasons, such as when they have a special interest in common. On such occasions small talk is not an important feature.

Visitors to the planet sometimes feel uncomfortable at the characteristically blunt and direct manner of the natives, but if they can get used to it, they often find it refreshing. For on this planet there is nothing hidden and no pretence. No one is treated in any way differently purely on account of his status. Compliments and insults alike are doled out with complete sincerity and openness and everyone knows exactly where he stands.

Emotions are expressed with equal openness, which allows them no time to fester. In consequence, there is no room at all for grudges, bitterness, resentment, hypocrisy or psychological 'game playing'.

Humour on this planet falls into two very distinct categories, neither of which is ever decadent or cruel. The first is an obvious and uncomplicated slapstick humour; the second a very sophisticated humour based on clever word play.

In every home and on every street corner, special destressing capsules are to be found that help deal with the exceptional sensitivities which are so common. These capsules work by allowing the user complete control over a simulated sensory environment – choosing his own level of light, colour, pressure, noise, and so on.

But perhaps the most special feature of all on Planet Asperger is the great respect given to children and their values. All its inhabitants grow up to adulthood without losing some of the more beautiful qualities of childhood – the sense of wonder, uncensored honesty and ability to see moral issues with uncompromising clarity.

Appendices

Applied Behaviour Analysis (ABA)

The PEAT Group

I came across Applied Behaviour Analysis (ABA) completely by accident just after my son was diagnosed with Asperger Syndrome. I happened to see a local newspaper article about a group of parents who were getting together in the University of Ulster to learn a way to manage behaviour in their autistic children. By that stage I had major problems managing my son's behaviour, so I went along with an open mind to see what I could learn.

The group was led by Dr Mickey Keenan and Dr Ken Kerr from the Psychology Department. These two men were passionately dedicated to the idea of teaching ABA to parents, to enable them to help their autistic children. They set up a charity known as PEAT (Parents' Education as Autism Therapists) and gave up a lot of their free time for no payment. Over the next few years I became involved with the PEAT group and learned all I could about ABA.

The other parents in the group were generally using ABA to teach their children very basic skills such as talking because their children had classic autism. To be honest I often felt like a bit of a misfit in the group because the challenges of an AS child are very different to those of a classically autistic child. But I remained involved because I was interested in the basic principles underlying ABA and I believed they could be successfully applied to a child with Asperger Syndrome.

ABA has helped me realise that although we cannot control anyone's behaviour except our own, we can do a lot to train a child's behaviour by how we respond to it. It's funny how your ideas change! I used to fondly imagine that 'behaviour training' had no part in bringing up children. But in fact we are doing it all the time, whether we realise it or not.

In my experience, although ABA has been very hard work, it has been a very successful and empowering tool. It has improved my son's motivation and helped him with many aspects of his behaviour. He took particularly well to the idea of the Token Economy (see Appendix 3). The big advantages were that it allowed him to be constructively involved and kept us both feeling we were on the same side.

Using ABA

It is beyond the scope of this book to go into ABA in any detail. The following brief overview is only meant to give a flavour of some of the principles and techniques.

Planning an ABA intervention (see also Appendix 2)

- Identify the target behaviour.

- What is the goal?

- What is the background to the behaviour problem?

- What is the justification for any intervention?

- Step 1: Perform an A–B–C.
  A–B–C stands for **A**ntecedent–**B**ehaviour–**C**onsequence. This step involves spending some time looking closely at the target behaviour itself, what preceded it and what the consequences were.

- Step 2: Analyse the A–B–C.

- Step 3: List some possible reinforcers and possible aversive consequences.

- Step 4: Translate the goal into an objective.

Planning an ABA Intervention

This is an example only, in order to illustrate in a step-by-step way how the principles of ABA might be used to plan an intervention. It is a real example, however, and resulted in 'The Clear Speech game' which is reproduced in Appendix 10, and which was used very successfully with my son.

DATE:_____

Target Behaviour

Unclear and idiosyncratic speech.

Goal

Clear speech.

Background

Kenneth is capable of speaking very well, but very often speaks unclearly or strangely, e.g. holding on to a syllable monotonously, mumbling quickly, or running all his words together so that even his close family cannot understand him. In social situations people often ask him to repeat himself. A typical response might be to refuse, mumble, or shout loudly, accusing the listener of not listening properly.

Justification

His communication and interpersonal skills should improve with clearer speech. There should be less frustration and fewer misunderstandings for everyone. I hope this will have a wider benefit, including helping his confidence and self-esteem.

Step 1: Perform an A–B–C

A–B–C done (see Appendix 1).

Step 2: Analyse the A–B–C

Analysis and conclusions

The following have an aversive effect:

- Complaining about not understanding him.
- Criticising, displaying impatience in manner and tone of voice.
- Asking him to repeat himself.

The following reinforce clear speech:

- Modelling exaggeratedly clear, distinct speech.
- Extravagant praise for his effort when he speaks clearly.

Step 3: List Possible Reinforcers and Possible Aversive Consequences

Consider how antecedents/consequences might be controlled.

Possible reinforcers

- Involve him as much as possible in planning a programme.
- Model desired behaviour as often as possible.

- Make it fun – make up a game.

- Have a clearly understood structure and realistic goals to encourage experience of fun and success.

- Lots of praise and encouragement for progress.

- Involve him in picking rewards for effort and progress through the programme.

Possible aversives

For deliberate non-compliance in the programme:

- Withdraw attention.

- Move on to less desirable activity.

- Token fine.

- Threaten sanction such as deducting TV time.

Step 4: Translate Goal into Objective(s)

Reminder: include an action verb phrase, conditions and criteria for acceptable performance.

Objectives

Speak in all situations including social, in such a way as to comply with the 'Clear Speech Rules' (see Appendix 10).

Eventual criterion for acceptable performance will be going a full day with no one asking him to repeat himself.

A Token Economy

The Principle

The child is motivated to improve his behaviour by having an alternative fun currency whereby he has the potential to 'earn' tokens by good behaviour or be 'fined' tokens for bad behaviour. He may then save the tokens or 'buy' prizes periodically from the Prize Store.

Developing Inner Motivation

A Token Economy is clearly a form of external motivation and ultimately the AS child will need to develop inner motivation as well. However a Token Economy can be used as a stepping stone to that end. Unless we have a way of kickstarting desirable behaviour, the child will never get the chance to experience the inner satisfaction of doing well just for its own sake.

When he behaves well, it is important to give him plenty of praise and encouragement for his efforts, along with the more tangible reward of tokens. This will encourage him to *link his good behaviour with both praise and tangible rewards* and he will come to see both of them as desirable. As he matures and grows in confidence, his inner motivation should develop and he can be weaned off the Token Economy.

How to Set Up a Token Economy

You will need tokens and a Prize Store.

Tokens could be counters or better still 'play money'.

About the Prize Store

1. Prizes need to be items that your child likes enough so that he is motivated to make an effort to earn them.

2. They should be bought in advance and stored in a specific area of the home which the child does not normally have access to. It could be anywhere – a box under a bed, a high cupboard, etc.

3. Obviously, don't spend more money than you can afford to build up the Prize Store. Look out for bargains and work within your own budget.

4. If you are thinking about giving your child a toy or treat for no particular reason, think sometimes about whether it could be put into the Prize Store instead.

5. Involve the child in building up the Prize Store by, for example:

   ○ getting his suggestions on new prizes (give him the fun of looking through catalogues)

   ○ showing him new prizes as you buy them (but not letting him open them!)

   ○ helping you to 'price' them.

6. To add value to Token Economy prizes, it is important that they should *only be available through the Token Economy*. The child should not be able to get them by any other means, or the prizes will become less valuable to him.

7. Prizes can of course also be non-material rewards such as a favourite outing or meal, etc.

Lucky Dips

As a special reward, give the child a Lucky Dip occasionally. This means he closes his eyes and dips in to a selection of prizes and is allowed to keep whatever prize he chooses.

Token Economy Pricelist

The following is a real example of a Token Economy pricelist. It might give you some ideas!

Books

Bart Simpson's Treehouse of Horror 1000 tokens

Small paperback books 150 tokens each

Confectionery

Chocolate coins 5 tokens each

Chocolate footballs 5 tokens each

Mallow cables 20 tokens each

Mints 5 tokens

Chocolate soldiers 10 tokens each

Toys, etc.

Cartoon maker 325 tokens

Compass 155 tokens

Electronic piano songbook 350 tokens

Kaleidoscope 160 tokens

Intruder alarm kit 1000 tokens

Invisible maze 200 tokens

Joke biscuits 200 tokens each

Joke file funfax 450 tokens

Mind teaser puzzles 150 tokens each/all 12 for 1200 tokens

Metal detector 1300 tokens

Papier mâché 600 tokens

Radiometer 800 tokens

Scallywags 325 tokens

Snake tin 400 tokens

Space ball 220 tokens

Zigzag spinning top game 800 tokens

Other prizes

Trip to zoo 250 tokens
Outing to science park 250 tokens
Video rental 250 tokens
Trip to animal sanctuary 250 tokens
Cinema visit 250 tokens
Mystery tour 250 tokens
Jammy day 250 tokens

Ground Rules

An example only

Date:_____

Rules

- You must always ask permission before watching TV or playing computer games.

- When you have homework to do, you must apply yourself to it properly for at least 20 minutes before 5 pm.

- You must have a shower every evening between 7.00 and 7.30 pm.

- You must not be violent to your sister (or anybody else).

Goals

- Treat other people the way you would like to be treated.

- Treat your own and other people's property with respect and take care not to damage it.

Allowances

- Daily TV/computer games: 1 hour.

- Weekly pocket money: £2.00.

Privileges

You are not automatically entitled to privileges. A privilege is something you need to *earn* (for example, by making extra effort with behaviour, or for lots of Happy Face ☺ behaviour.) It will normally be negotiated with parents in advance. A privilege could be for example:

- Extra pocket money.
- Being allowed Pringles and coke in your bedroom.
- Extra TV/computer time.
- A special treat such as, for example, sweets, cake, a special outing, a comic, a toy, game or book.

Sanctions

- A sanction can be given if your behaviour is not up to the required standard. Parents will try to make sure you always know what that standard is.
- We will always try to give you a warning before any sanction, *unless we judge that your behaviour is very serious, dangerous or deliberately defiant.*
- A sanction could be, for example, a Token Fine, withdrawal or reduction of a privilege or, for more serious behaviour, the withdrawal of an allowance.

My Emotions Book

This is an example to give suggestions of content, etc.

About Feelings

Everyone has emotions or feelings. There are many kinds of feelings. The main ones are:

- Happy
- Sad
- Angry
- Frightened

Everyone has different things that can make them feel happy, sad, angry or afraid.

About Me

The colour that makes me feel most happy is:

- Blue

A colour that I don't like is:

- Pink

My favourite TV show is:

- Simpsons

My Happy Pages

Here are some things that make me feel happy:

- Chocolate

- Pringles

- Enid Blyton books

Here are some pictures and photos that make me feel happy:

My Sad Pages

Here are some things that make me feel sad:

- People teasing me

- Animals being hunted

Here are some pictures and photos that make me feel sad:

My Angry Pages

Here are some things that make me feel angry:

- Somebody hitting me

- Somebody breaking my toys

Here are some pictures and photos that make me feel angry:

My Frightened Pages

Here are some things that make me feel frightened:

- A big storm

- A scarey movie

Here are some pictures and photos that make me feel frightened:

About Other People's Feelings

Other people have different emotions. I did an interview with Granny to find out about her emotions.

About Granny

The colour that makes Granny feel most happy is:

- Red

A colour that Granny doesn't like is:

- Purple

Granny's favourite TV show is:

- Granny doesn't like very many TV shows these days

Granny's Happy Pages

Here are some things that make Granny feel happy:

- Knitting

- Seeing old friends

- Her grandchildren giving her a hug

- Me being friendly to her

Granny's Sad Pages

Here are some things that make Granny feel sad:

- To see her family being hurt

- Thinking about some people who have died

Granny's Angry Pages

Here are some things that make Granny feel angry:

- Somebody unravelling her knitting

Granny's frightened pages

Here are some things that make Granny feel frightened:

- A scary movie
- The sea

Some Ways I can make Granny Happy

- Giving her a hug
- Being friendly to her

Anger Dos and Don'ts

(Example only)

About Feeling Angry

Everybody feels angry sometimes. It's OK to feel angry but some angry behaviour is not OK. When I am angry I can make choices about how I behave. It is OK to choose to do something from the *Anger Do* list, but it is not OK to choose to do something from the *Anger Don't* list.

Anger Dos

- Punch a punchbag.
- Draw or scribble with crayons on paper.
- Pummel a pillow.
- Talk to an adult about how I feel.
- Have a joke.
- Go for a run around the garden.

Anger Don'ts

- Hit people.
- Keep my feelings locked inside.
- Throw things.
- Sulk.

- Shout and yell at people.
- Tease other people.
- Damage or destroy things.

Emotion Vocabulary

Happy words

Comfortable
Delighted
Ecstatic
Elated
Excited
Fulfilled
Glad
Jolly
Joyful
Merry
Pleased
Positive
Proud
Purposeful
Reassured
Relaxed
Relieved
Safe
Secure
Successful
Thankful

Sad words

Alienated
Alone
Betrayed
Depressed
Despairing
Devastated
Disappointed
Displeased
Distressed
Frustrated
Grieving
Inferior
Isolated
Jealous
Lonely
Lost
Low
Miserable
Rejected
Tearful
Unwanted
Weepy

Angry words

Bad tempered
Confused
Crazy
Cross
Demented
Distrustful
Furious
Hostile
Hysterical
In a fog
Insane
Mad
Numb
Out of control
Paranoid
Raging
Suspicious

Frightened words

Afraid
Agitated
Alarmed
Anxious
Apprehensive
Distressed
Fearful
Frightened
Guilty
Nervous
Panicky
Scared
Shaky
Shy
Tense
Terrified
Timid
Troubled
Wobbly
Worried

Ways To Earn
Happy Faces ☺ and Sad Faces ☹

(Example only)

I can earn Happy Faces ☺ by:

Co-operation ☺

Consideration ☺

Courtesy ☺

Effort ☺

Friendliness ☺

Gentleness ☺

Helpfulness ☺

Joyfulness ☺

Kindness ☺

Patience ☺

Perseverence ☺

Pleasant tone of voice ☺

Positive attitude ☺

Self-control ☺

Singing ☺

Smiles ☺

I can earn Sad Faces ☹ by:

Aggression ☹

Arguing ☹

Cheek ☹

Complaints ☹ (suggestions are OK!)

Contradicting ☹ (ditto)

Criticism ☹ (ditto)

Demands ☹ (polite requests are OK)

Disobeying ☹

Disrespecting ☹

Ignoring requests, etc. ☹

Rudeness ☹

Sarcasm ☹

Shouting rudely or impatiently ☹

Verbal bullying ☹

Breaking a Task into Smaller Steps

(Example only)

Showering Reminder Card

1. Undress.

2. Put clothes away neatly.

3. Have clothes/pyjamas, etc. ready for after.

4. Check shower dial position and adjust if necessary.

5. Check sprayhead position and adjust if necessary.

6. Remove sprayhead and hold away from self in one hand.

7. Turn on shower and let it run for a few moments for temperature to settle (adjust if necessary).

8. Mount sprayhead back onto holder.

9. Stand under water spray and get soaked! Use soap/shampoo, etc. to wash all of body (and hair) not missing any (sponge/flannel can be used if preferred).

10. Rinse thoroughly until soap all washed off.

11. Turn off shower and get out.

12. Towel dry body and hair.

13. Dress/pyjamas.

14. Comb hair into shape.

15. Dry with hairdryer.

The Clear Speech Game

This is a game for 2 players. You will need counters and a beanbag. The winner is the player with the most counters at the end.

How to Play

1. A pile of counters and a beanbag are put in the middle.

2. The players sit facing each other.

3. The timer is set for the agreed time.

4. During the agreed time (three minutes to start with), the players must have a conversation. It can be a spontaneous conversation, or else a topic can be agreed upon before the game starts.

5. *During the conversation players must carefully observe the CLEAR SPEECH RULES* (see below).

6. You are only allowed to take your turn in the conversation while you are holding the beanbag.

7. When you have finished speaking, you must pass it to the other player.

8. Every time you pass, you take a counter from the middle and make a pile.

Challenging

While one player is speaking, the other player listens carefully and may *challenge* (by calling out 'CHALLENGE!') at any time on the grounds that one or more of the CLEAR SPEECH RULES has been broken. The players then take a moment to discuss which rule or rules have been broken. Both players must be honest and decide whether it is a fair and reasonable challenge: if they want they can do a 'replay' by repeating the part of the conversation that gave rise to the challenge, this time without breaking any of the rules. If a player makes a successful challenge, he takes an extra counter from the pile in the middle and adds it to his own pile. Play then resumes.

Ending the Game

Play finishes when there are no counters left, or the time allowed for playing the game is up.

The Clear Speech Rules

- *Volume:* not speaking too loudly or too quietly.
- *Fluency:* not hesitating too much.
- *Rate:* not speaking too quickly or too slowly.
- *Clarity:* speaking clearly, not mumbling.
- *Intonation:* sounding interesting, not boring.
- *Manners:* speaking politely.
- *Grammar:* using correct grammar.

Hurting is Not Always Intentional

Checklist

Because the AS child has little awareness of the intentions of other people, it can be hard for him to tell the difference between bullying and unintentional hurt. Use this checklist to help you identify gaps in his awareness on this point. Does he understand the following:

- He can hurt other people without intending to.

- Other people can hurt him without intending to.

- It can be hard to tell whether someone has hurt another person on purpose but there are ways to try and find out.

- His feelings are very important and if he feels hurt he is entitled to feel that way.

- If you know that someone did not mean to hurt you, it might not stop you feeling bad but at least it can help a bit.

Suggested Discussion Points

It is not always easy to know where the gaps in his awareness lie. Look for opportunities to talk to him as a way of finding out what his level of understanding really is. What he says may be very revealing. It can also be useful to include other family members in chats and discussions as appropriate. Here are some examples of the kinds of questions you could ask your child as a way of opening up a discussion:

- Can people hurt each other without intending to?

- How might this happen?

- Might you have ever hurt someone without intending to?

- Do you think someone has ever hurt you without intending to?

- How might you be able to tell whether someone intended to hurt you?

- If someone hurts another person by accident, does this mean they don't have to apologise or make amends?

What the AS Child May Need to be Told

1. People often hurt each other without intending to. Sometimes you might upset someone without intending to. And sometimes when you feel upset by another person he may not have intended any harm either.

2. If you are not sure whether someone has intended to hurt or upset you, perhaps you could ask him directly. Or perhaps you could talk the matter over with an adult or friend that you trust.

3. When someone realises he has hurt another person – even unintentionally – it is good manners for him to apologise anyway. He might also try to make amends in some way.

Examples You Could Use to Help Him Understand

Here are two examples of situations where you might feel hurt and angry by someone's behaviour and where it is hard to tell whether the other person intends to hurt you:

- Someone breaks or damages your belongings.

- Someone hurts your toe by standing on it.

In each of these cases the person *may have intended to cause you hurt*. It might be:

- He is deliberately trying to annoy you just to be mean or because he is on bad form.

- He is trying to get back at you because he feels upset at something you did which annoyed and provoked him.

- He is trying to provoke you to misbehave and get you into trouble.

On the other hand the person *may not have intended to cause you hurt*. It might be:

- He dropped one of your toys by accident and it broke and he is very sorry about it.

- He stood on your foot accidentally. Perhaps he was not watching where he was going.

Teasing and Banter

Checklist

How much do you feel your child knows and understands? Use this checklist to help you identify gaps in his understanding about teasing and the ways in which teasing is different from bullying. Does he understand:

- People sometimes tease by making fun of other people.

- Sometimes this is meant to cause hurt.

- Sometimes it is meant as a joke.

- Sometimes people take teasing the wrong way.

- Sometimes people hurt each other without meaning to when they tease. They may not even realise that they have caused offence.

- There are ways to try and find out whether someone is joking or whether he is trying to be hurtful when they tease.

Suggested Discussion Points

It is not always easy to know where the gaps in his awareness lie. Look for opportunities to talk to him as a way of finding out what his level of understanding really is. What he says may be very revealing. It can also be useful to include other family members in chats and discussions as appropriate. Here are some examples of the kinds of questions you could ask your child as a way of opening up a discussion:

- Is teasing always meant to be cruel?
- How can you tell if someone is only joking?
- When is teasing OK and when is it not OK?
- Do you understand what 'banter' is?
- How does the dictionary define 'banter'?
- Can you think of any examples of teasing and banter?

What the AS Child May Need to be Told

1. Teasing happens when someone amuses himself by deliberately making fun of another person. This kind of thing goes on a lot and so it is hard to avoid.

2. It can feel very hurtful and embarrassing to be on the receiving end of this kind of treatment. For example, your brother or a child in school might call you a silly name like 'monkey face'. He might find this very amusing but if you do not see the funny side you can end up feeling embarrassed hurt and angry.

3. People tease for different reasons. Sometimes people who are being mean tease in order deliberately to embarrass and hurt other people. This can be a form of bullying. But although teasing can feel bad *it is not always meant to be cruel*. The teaser may have meant his comment as a joke and imagined you would have found it funny too.

4. *Friendly* joking and teasing is sometimes called 'banter'. Banter goes on a lot, especially among good friends and family members. It can be a way of having some innocent fun together.

5. It is very hard to tell whether or not someone is intending to be cruel when they tease but it is helpful to keep in mind:

- If the teaser is a genuinely friendly person and they are smiling when they make the comment there is a good chance that they are only joking.

- A mean person or false friend is likely to want to hurt people on purpose. And remember, a mean person or false friend is the type of person who:

    — does not treat you as well as he treats his other friends

    — notices your mistakes and embarrasses you by drawing them to the attention of others

    — threatens not to be your friend unless you do what he wants rather than what you feel comfortable with

    — seems to want to put you down all the time.

What is Bullying?

Checklist

How much do you feel your child knows and understands about bullying? Use this checklist to help you identify gaps in his awareness. Does he understand:

- Bullying is mean and unacceptable behaviour.
- It can be very hurtful.
- There are many different kinds of bullying.
- No kind of bullying is ever OK.
- It should always be reported.
- Adults will do all in their power to take it seriously and deal with it.
- No one deserves to be bullied.

Suggested Discussion Points

It is not always easy to know where the gaps in his awareness lie. Look for opportunities to talk to him as a way of finding out what his level of understanding really is. What he says may be very revealing. It can also be useful to include other family members in chats and discussions as appropriate. Here are some examples of the kinds of questions you could ask your child as a way of opening up a discussion:

- Can you think of any examples of bullying and mean behaviour?
- Have there been times when you have felt bullied?

- Do you think you ever bullied someone yourself?
- Does bullying always have to be physical?
- Is bullying ever OK?

What the as child may need to be told

Bullying happens when a person says or does something to hurt or frighten another person or to make him feel bad. Physical bullying might happen when someone hurts your body or damages your belongings, but bullying is not always physical. Bullying should never be tolerated. Here are some examples of bullying behaviour.

Physical bullying

- hitting
- kicking
- pinching
- biting
- pushing and shoving
- damaging belongings
- stealing.

Other examples of bullying

- Saying or writing mean or nasty things about another person.
- Making threats.
- Spreading nasty rumours.
- Encouraging you to do things which get you into trouble.
- Mimicking the way a person speaks.
- Name calling.

- Ignoring.

- Excluding, for example, leaving a child out of a game.

- Forcing another person to do things he does not really want to do.

- Doing mean things when the teacher or adult in charge is not looking.

- Cruel nasty teasing, for example, about a person's size or handwriting.

Bullying Dos and Don'ts

Do

- Remember if someone is bullying you it is not your fault.
- Tell what has happened to a trustworthy adult like a parent or teacher.
- If it is helpful, take a trustworthy friend with you to help report what has happened.
- Walk away quickly and calmly and seek help.
- If you are worried about being bullied by other children while you are on a bus, try to sit near the driver or other adults.
- If you see bullying going on, report it and seek help.
- Remember bullying is wrong and reporting it is *not* 'telling tales'.

Don't

- Show the person who is hurting you that you are upset. (This is very difficult to do.)
- React in an angry or aggressive way. If you hit out you may end up getting yourself into trouble.

Useful Websites

Applied Behaviour Analysis (ABA)
www.helpuslearn.com

AS and proud of it
www.AS-and-Proud-of-it@onelist.com

Aspergers Syndrome Education Network
www.aspennj.org

Tony Attwood
www.tonyattwood.com

Autism Research Centre
www.psychiatry.cam.uk

Bullying Online
www.bullying.co.uk

National Autistic Society
www.oneworld.org

Oops Wrong Planet! Syndrome
(includes link to Autism Spectrum e-mail penpal registry)
www.isn.net

University Students with Autism and Aspergers Syndrome
www.cns.dicon.co.uk

Bibliography

Alston, J. and Taylor, J. (1995) *Handwriting Helpline.* Manchester: Dextral Books.

Anderson, E. and Emmons, P. (1996) *Unlocking the Mysteries of Sensory Dysfunction.* Arlington, TX: Future Horizons.

Attwood, T. (1998) *Asperger's Syndrome.* London: Jessica Kingsley Publishers.

Baron-Cohen, S. (1997) *Mindblindness.* Cambridge, MA: MIT Press.

Bridge, S. (1995) *The Art of Imperfect Parenting.* London: Hodder and Stoughton.

Chalke, S. (1997) *How to Succeed as a Parent.* London: Hodder and Stoughton.

Durand, V.M. (1998) *Sleep Better.* Baltimore, MD: Brookes.

Faber, A. and Mazlish, E. (1982) *How to Talk so Kids Will Listen and Listen So Kids Will Talk.* New York: Avon Books.

Fling, E.R. (2000) *Eating an Artichoke.* London: Jessica Kingsley Publishers.

Frith, U. (1991) *Autism and Asperger Syndrome.* Cambridge: Cambridge University Press.

Goleman, D. (1996) *Emotional Intelligence.* London: Bloomsbury.

Grandin, T. (1995) *Thinking in Pictures.* London: Vintage.

Hall, K. (2000) *Asperger Syndrome, the Universe and Everything.* London: Jessica Kingsley Publishers.

Holt, J. (1982) *Teach Your Own.* Hants: Lighthouse Books.

Howlin, P., Baron-Cohen, S. and Hadwin, J. (1999) *Teaching Children with Autism to Mind Read.* Chichester: Wiley.

Jones, C. Folz (1994) *Mistakes that Worked.* New York: Doubleday.

Keenan, M., Kerr, K. and Dillenburger, K. (2000) *Parents' Education as Autism Therapists.* London: Jessica Kingsley Publishers.

Legge, B. (2002) *Can't Eat, Won't Eat.* London: Jessica Kingsley Publishers.

Makin, P.E. and Lindley, P. (1991) *Positive Stress Management.* London: Kogan Page.

Miltenberger, R. (1997) *Behaviour Modification.* London: Brookes/Cole.

Nierenberg, G. and Calero, H. (1980) *How to Read a Person like a Book.* London: Thorsons.

O'Neill, J.L. (eds) (1999) *Through the Eyes of Aliens.* London: Jessica Kingsley Publishers.

Smith Myles, B. and Southwick, J (1999) *Asperger Syndrome and Difficult Moments.* Shawnee Mission, KS: Autism Asperger Publishing Co.

Willey, L.H. (1999) *Pretending to be Normal.* London: Jessica Kingsley Publishers.

Tip Finder

A List of All the Ideas, Tips
and Strategies Contained in the Book

I Laying the Foundations

Looking After Yourself (pages 15–21)

1. Keep yourself stocked up (the 'Freezer Tip!')
2. Get plenty of support
3. Don't take things personally
4. Don't neglect other areas of your life
5. Be realistic about tackling problems
6. Give yourself SMART goals
7. Let the strategies be 'on tap' not 'on top'
8. Try not to spoil him
9. Find someone talk to
10. Mums – let yourself off the hook
11. 'Mind over matter!'

Acceptance and Understanding (pages 21–27)

12. Accept the diagnosis
13. Find out more about Asperger Syndrome
14. Can't versus won't?
15. Understand his rigidity (trains versus cars)
16. Investigate the reasons for poor behaviour
17. 'Make friends before you make points'
18. Be on his side

Building Self-Esteem (pages 27–30)

19. 'Catch him doing something right'
20. Reward rather than punish
21. Have 'Positive Sessions'
22. Help him avoid humiliation
23. Involve him in behaviour planning

Reducing Anxiety (pages 30–38)

Understand and make allowances

24. Be aware of 'hidden anxiety'
25. Investigate the reasons
26. Aim for an optimum level of anxiety

Provide order, structure and predictability

27. Time any changes carefully
28. Use a noticeboard
29. Use a timer or stopwatch
30. Use visual aids
31. Laminate the visual aids

A few other suggestions

2 Bringing Out the Best in Your Child

Bridging the Social and Emotional Gap (pages 39–50)

Developing his awareness: some techniques to try

Developing his awareness: some activities and games to try

Play and social skills: some ideas to try

The Best Approach (pages 51–55)

Encouraging Compliance and Motivation (pages 56–59)

To encourage compliance

To increase motivation

Dealing with Difficult Moments (pages 59–62)

3 Common Problems A–Z

Anger and Aggression (pages 64–69)

Ideas for dealing with a crisis (see also tips 71–77, dealing with difficult moments)

83. Have a Crisis Plan
84. Nip explosive situations in the bud
85. Stay calm
86. Don't give in to intimidation
87. Let him play to an empty stage

Attention Difficulties (pages 70–75)

88. Make instructions very specific
89. Don't overload him
90. Write things down and use 'visual aids'
91. Get him a scheduler or organiser

Ideas to help him focus on a task

92. Remove distractions
93. Use the 'When…then' formula
94. Time planning
95. Progress Cards

Bedtime and Sleeping (pages 76–79)

96. Reduce anxiety during the day
97. Establish a bedtime routine
98. Display the evening routine
99. Make sure his room isn't too bright
100. Have a 'Positive Session'
101. Use an evening alarm clock
102. Make a special tape
103. Use lavender

Depression (pages 80–83)

104. Be vigilant
105. Lay a loving foundation
106. Give him time
107. Empathic listening
108. Help him feel successful
109. Protect him where he needs protection
110. Seek medical help when appropriate

Food Issues (pages 84–90)

For the faddy eater

111. Make him simple food
112. Small portions
113. Incentives for after meals
114. Purée soups
115. Give supplements

For the overeater

116. A structured food allowance

Ideas to help either problem

117. Exercise
118. Regular mealtimes
119. Take the pressure off
120. Persevere
121. Involve him in food preparation
122. A Food Progress list
123. Meal planning
124. Seek expert help

Handwriting (pages 91–96)

125. Practise little and often
126. Find a purpose
127. Use attractive writing materials
128. Model slow careful writing
129. 'The quick brown fox'
130. Blank pages and double-spacing
131. Seek expert help if needed

Activities and games to encourage handwriting

132. Have a contest
133. Puzzle books
134. Paper and pencil games
135. 'Dummy's Meeting'
136. Treasure hunt

Homework Supervision (pages 97–98)

Provide structure

137. Prepare
138. Take charge
139. Provide a very structured setting
140. Use the 'When…then' formula

Motor Skills and Co-ordination (pages 99–102)

141. Nurture his strengths
142. Make it fun
143. Make it a challenge
144. Expert help if needed

Games and activities

145.   Beanbag games

146.   Obstacle course

147.   Cross-stitch

Perfectionism (pages 103–109)

148.   Teach him 'Smart Thinking' about mistakes

149.   Encourage and praise effort rather than outcome

150.   Help him to be a good sport

151.   Model making mistakes

152.   Have a 'Mistake Confession Session'

153.   Make up some family mottos

154.   Encourage a healthy self-esteem

Rigidity (pages 110–114)

155.   Remember how hard it is for him to be flexible

156.   Keep him informed but don't mislead

157.   Reduce anxiety

158.   Gradually encourage flexibility

School Issues (pages 115–128)

159.   Choosing the most suitable school

160.   Prepare and equip him

161.   Be vigilant

162.   Make home a safe haven

163.   Keep communication lines open

164.   Liaise with the professionals

165.   Ability and attainment assessments

166.   Dealing with the problem of bullying

167.   Approaching the school about bullying

168.   Give him 'time out'

Sensory Issues (pages 129–134)

Some games to play

Special Events, Social Occasions and Outings (pages 135–142)

Ideas for the car journey

Speech and Conversation (pages 143–148)

Some games and activities